Entrepreneurship Research: Past Perspectives and Future Prospects

Entrepreneurship Research: Past Perspectives and Future Prospects

Anders Lundström

*President, The Swedish Foundation for
Small Business Research (FSF)
S-701 82 Örebro, Sweden
lundstrom@fsf.se*

Sune Halvarsson

*Deputy General Director, The Swedish Agency for
Economic and Regional Growth (NUTEK)
117 86 Stockholm, Sweden
Sune.halvarsson@nutek.se*

now

the essence of knowledge

Boston – Delft

Foundations and Trends® in Entrepreneurship

Published, sold and distributed by:
now Publishers Inc.
PO Box 1024
Hanover, MA 02339
USA
Tel. +1-781-985-4510
www.nowpublishers.com
sales@nowpublishers.com

Outside North America:
now Publishers Inc.
PO Box 179
2600 AD Delft
The Netherlands
Tel. +31-6-51115274

Library of Congress Control Number: 2006935706

The preferred citation for this publication is A. Lundström and S. Halvarsson, Entrepreneurship Research: Past Perspectives and Future Prospects, Foundations and Trends® in Entrepreneurship, vol 2, no 3, pp 145–259, 2006

Printed on acid-free paper

ISBN: 1-933019-35-2
© 2006 A. Lundström and S. Halvarsson

Foundations and Trends® in Entrepreneurship
Volume 2 Issue 3, 2006
Editorial Board

Editorial Scope

Foundations and Trends® in Entrepreneurship will publish survey and tutorial articles in the following topics:

- Nascent and start-up entrepreneurs
- Opportunity recognition
- New venture creation process
- Business formation
- Firm ownership
- Market value and firm growth
- Franchising
- Managerial characteristics and behavior of entrepreneurs
- Strategic alliances and networks
- Government programs and public policy
- Gender and ethnicity
- New business financing:

- Business angels
- Bank financing, debt, and trade credit
- Venture capital and private equity capital
- Public equity and IPO’s
- Family-owned firms
- Management structure, governance and performance
- Corporate entrepreneurship
- High technology
- Technology-based new firms
- High-tech clusters
- Small business and economic growth

Information for Librarians

Foundations and Trends® in Entrepreneurship, 2006, Volume 2, 4 issues. ISSN paper version 1551-3114. ISSN online version 1551-3122. Also available as a combined paper and online subscription.

Foundations and Trends® in
Entrepreneurship
Vol. 2, No 3 (2006) 145–259
© 2006 A. Lundström and S. Halvarsson
DOI: 10.1561/0300000009

Entrepreneurship Research: Past Perspectives and Future Prospects

Anders Lundström[1] and Sune Halvarsson[2]

[1] President, The Swedish Foundation for Small Business Research (FSF),
lundstrom@fsf.se

[2] Deputy General Director, The Swedish Agency for Economic and Regional
Growth (NUTEK), Sune.halvarsson@nutek.se

Abstract

Since 1996 the Swedish Foundation for Small Business Research (FSF)
and the Swedish National Board for Industrial and Technical Development (NUTEK) have been rewarding research on small business and
entrepreneurship with the FSF–NUTEK Award for research on small
business and entrepreneurship. This award is given to leading scholars
who have had the greatest impact in shaping the field of small business
and entrepreneurship research. In particular, FSF and NUTEK invited
these pre-eminent scholars of entrepreneurship to share their views,
insights and expertise on where the field of entrepreneurship and small
business research is coming from and where it is heading. The articles contained in this 10th-year Anniversary Issue of *Foundations and
Trends in Entrepreneurship* reflects the best of the best of scholarship
in the field of entrepreneurship and small business research.

Contents

1

Introduction

Since 1996 the Swedish Foundation for Small Business Research (FSF) and the Swedish National Board for Industrial and Technical Development (NUTEK) have been rewarding research on small business and entrepreneurship with the FSF–NUTEK Award for research on small business and entrepreneurship. This award is given to leading scholars who have had the greatest impact in shaping the field of small business and entrepreneurship research. The award was made on the basis of meticulous scrutiny of leading scholars in entrepreneurship and small business all around the world. The final recommendations and selection are made by a highly qualified panel of experts. The award winners span a broad spectrum of academic fields and disciplines, ranging from management to economics, sociology, and political science to regional science. Information concerning the award along with a list of the winners can be found at http://www.fsf.se/fsf-nutek-award/winners.htm

The ambition behind the award was and remains threefold:

(1) to highlight the importance of research that is being produced in the areas of entrepreneurship and small business;

(2) to further stimulate and promote scholarly work within these
     fields of research;

(3) to diffuse the state-of-the art research among scholars, prac-
     titioners, and people involved in small business development.

Since then, this research field has generated increasing interest and
the issues are constantly being given greater importance on the agenda.
We at the FSF and NUTEK are very proud to look back at these
10 years of rewarding outstanding research, and confident that the
research awarded has contributed to our increased understanding of
the small business sector and entrepreneurship in general.

While celebrating the 10th-year anniversary, it is natural to look
back and reflect on the past for just a moment. Still, we at FSF
and NUTEK opted to approach our 10th-year anniversary by looking ahead. We asked each award-winner about their view on the future
of this research field. In particular, FSF and NUTEK invited these
pre-eminent scholars of entrepreneurship to share their views, insights,
and expertise on where the field of entrepreneurship and small business research is coming from and where it is heading. The articles contained in this 10th-year Anniversary Issue of *Foundations and Trends
in Entrepreneurship* reflect the best of the scholarship in the field of
entrepreneurship and small business research.

Included in this volume of *Foundations and Trends in Entrepreneurship* as an insightful overview of how entrepreneurship as a scholarly
field of research has evolved over time by Arnold C. Cooper of Pur-
due University, "The Development of the Field of Entrepreneurship."
According to William J. Baumol of New York University, scholarship is
now coalescing into an academic field, as he argues in "Entrepreneurship and Small Business: Toward a Program of Research." David B.
Audretsch of the Max Planck Institute explains the interest, importance, and significance of the coalescing scholarly field of entrepreneurship as reflecting the shift from the managed economy to "The
Entrepreneurial Society." Charles Sabel of Columbia University focuses
on the issue of geography and the spatial role of entrepreneurship in
asking, "What to Make of the Changes in Industrial Districts? Three
Questions." A more historic view of scholarship on small business and

entrepreneurship is provided by Giacomo Becattini in "Some Notes on the Empirical Basis of the Role Attributed to Small business and Entrepreneurship in the Thought of Alfred Marshall."

Howard E. Aldrich of the University of North Carolina offers his views and insights on "Trends and Directions in Entrepreneurship Research." David Birch reflects on entrepreneurship research to address the question, "What Have We Learned?" Paul Reynolds offers insights into "Understanding Entrepreneurship: Achievements and Opportunities – A Personal Assessment." In "A Critical Mess Approach to Entrepreneurship Scholarship," William Gartner tries to make sense of a disparate and evolving literature on entrepreneurship.

Three of the prize-winners provide explicit views and insights into public policy toward entrepreneurship. In "A Formulation of Entrepreneurship Policy," Zoltan J. Acs of George Mason University explains how and why philanthropy plays a key role in linking entrepreneurship to economic growth. Similarly, Ian C. MacMillan of the Wharton School at the University of Pennsylvania focuses on "Social Wealth Creation via Experimental Entrepreneurial Philanthropy." Finally, David Storey of the Warwick Business School provides an overview of "Public Policy on Entrepreneurship and SMEs in Recent Years."

We hope that these state-of-the art insights into exciting ideas and reflections in the area of small business and entrepreneurship research will prove to be as rewarding to you as they are to us at the FSF and NUTEK.

2

The Development of the Field of Entrepreneurship

A. C. Cooper

There has been enormous growth in the academic field of entrepreneurship. This has been reflected in number of courses; Landstrom reported 2200 just in the United States (Landstrom, 2005, p. 4). It is also evident in the number of university-based centers for entrepreneurship (more than 90), chaired professorships (more than 400), and academic journals (more than 40) (Katz, 2005). These statistics primarily reflect developments in the United States. There have been, of course, similar developments in many other countries (Landstrom, 2005, pp. 95–129). Most of this development has occurred in the past 20–25 years, about half of a professional's working life.

Will entrepreneurship continue to be a vital and growing part of universities? Or will it be a field which flourished for a time and then was replaced by the next "hot topic"?

Much will depend on what happens outside of universities. If, for whatever reasons, entrepreneurship lessens or seems to offer poorer rewards, then student interest will decline. However in those societies in which entrepreneurship flourishes, going beyond self-employment ventures to growth-oriented firms, there will be widespread interest in the topic. In such settings, university students will be strongly motivated to develop the skills and knowledge which might permit them to become entrepreneurs, to work with or in entrepreneurial firms, or to be internal entrepreneurs within established corporations. To date, much of the growth in courses and programs has been driven by student demand and future growth will depend on whether students are excited by the subject and wish to study it.

For entrepreneurship education to flourish, the courses must be perceived as offering real value. This means that the intellectual-base of the field must continue to be developed. Good teaching materials must be prepared. Relevant theoretical frameworks and empirical findings from allied disciplines, such as sociology, economics, and psychology, should be drawn on and applied to questions relating to entrepreneurship. Scholars in related fields, such as finance, strategy, and organizational behavior, can address questions that are relevant to their fields and also to entrepreneurship.

The advances in the field will be driven primarily by the young faculties devoting their full attention to the field. Historically, part-time faculties have done much of the entrepreneurship teaching at many American universities, including some of those where we might expect cutting edge research to occur. These people are often fine teachers, but their background and training are such that they are unlikely to contribute to the research-base of the field. In addition, some of the full-time faculties who have taught entrepreneurship have made their primary research contributions in other fields, often earlier in their careers. Furthermore, some of the faculties attracted to the field have been of a practical bent, with stronger inclinations to be involved in entrepreneurship than to engage in studying it in a systematic way. Thus, the sociology of the field, the kinds of people who have provided much of the instruction, has made for interesting teaching, but slower development of the body of systematic research which should be at the core of an emerging field. As the research-base of entrepreneurship increases, universities are more likely to feel that they need to have full-time research-oriented faculties in the area and this, in turn, will accelerate the development of the field.

What has been the nature of development in the field to date and what are likely to be future patterns of development? Howard Aldrich suggested three possible paths of development. One path is that of a "normal science," with an accumulation of empirically tested hypotheses and well-grounded generalizations in what might increasingly be viewed as a specialized field. A second path is a multi-paradigm view, in which concepts from a variety of fields might be applied. In this view, theories and research methods might be borrowed from relevant fields and research might be published in the journals of those fields. A third approach is less theory-driven and more pragmatic. Topics might be chosen because of data availability and perceived usefulness (Aldrich and Baker, 2005).

As we consider development to this point, we can see that concepts from allied fields have been applied extensively to research relating to entrepreneurship. For instance, concepts and methods relating to network analysis have been borrowed from sociology, and theories from cognitive psychology have been applied to entrepreneurial cognition. In that sense, the field has become more multidisciplinary. There are also indications that questions relating to entrepreneurship are being pursued by scholars in other fields. The population ecology literature represents a well-defined stream of research initially developed by organizational sociologists, who have also done extensive work in examining the role of social capital in entrepreneurial ventures. The field of finance now has regular conferences of scholars doing work on venture finance and marketing has had a marketing and entrepreneurship conference for many years.

Relatively little research relating to entrepreneurship has been published in major general management journals. Busenitz et al., reported on a study of 5291 articles published in seven major general management journals over a 15-year period. They found only 1.8% of those articles related to entrepreneurship (Busenitz et al.). A search in June 2005 utilizing the Social Sciences Citation Index found more than 2400 articles relating in some way to entrepreneurship. Many were published in the specialized entrepreneurship journals, and very few were in the leading journals of sociology, economics, and psychology. Thus, we could say that the study of entrepreneurship has become more multidisciplinary in the concepts and methodologies it utilizes. However, most of the work in entrepreneurship has been presented in the specialized conferences and journals of the entrepreneurship field.

Has entrepreneurship made progress toward becoming a "normal science"? The work is more cumulative than in earlier years, but much more remains to be done. The boundaries of the field are porous and a variety of definitions continue to be drawn on in defining the field. Statistic methodologies are more sophisticated than in prior years. However, issues of validity and reliability have often received little attention. One would have to say that the field is not yet a normal science in the sense of having a well-defined body of research with its own theoretical frameworks and methodologies.

There continues to be a stream of writing which represents Aldrich's third path of development. These practitioner-oriented articles sometimes reflect formal research and sometimes represent the accumulated wisdom of the authors. Most entrepreneurship scholars are in business schools, where there has been a long-standing tradition of developing books and articles which are relevant and useful to practicing managers. We might note also that some entrepreneurship faculties are among those with the most applied orientation among business school faculties.

What are likely patterns of development for entrepreneurship research in the future? I would expect that research will continue to draw on concepts and methodologies from other fields. The field is likely to demonstrate increasing sophistication in its methodologies. There will also be a continuing stream of wisdom-based practitioner-oriented articles. However, I do not expect that there will be a single dominant paradigm in the near future.

What are some of the topics which future research is likely to explore? One way to think about this is to consider certain broad headings under which research might be organized. Any list would be incomplete, but here are some promising areas for future research.

Entrepreneur(s)

1) The human capital of the entrepreneur could be examined in more fine-grained ways. For instance, how do particular kinds of education or experience bear upon the likelihood of becoming an entrepreneur or how do they bear upon new venture success?
2) The cognitive processes of entrepreneurs, as they identify opportunities or as they form and manage their firms, could be explored in greater depth. Are certain cognitive processes associated with particular ways of starting or specific kinds of firms? Are they associated with particular patterns of success? Do cognitive processes tend to vary according to environmental characteristics, for instance the speed of change?
3) Entrepreneurial teams are important for growth-oriented firms, yet have received little attention. What factors bear upon the processes by which teams are formed? How do teams differ in the ways in which they function? Are these differences related to performance? How does the addition or departure of team members bear upon the internal dynamics of teams?

Role of incubator organizations

1) Why do some established organizations, which might be thought of as incubators, have higher spin-off rates of entrepreneurs than others? Why do some departments within established organizations have high spin-off rates and other departments have few or no entrepreneurs leaving?
2) How do the characteristics of different types of established organizations bear upon the strategies, resource positions, and prospects for success of spin-off firms? How do entrepreneurial ventures differ, depending on whether they spin off from non-profits (such as universities or hospitals), from government laboratories, or from corporations? How does the size of the established organization relate to the

strategies of the new firms or the nature of the management practices they put into effect?

3) Do established organizations in complexes of similar firms tend to have different rates or kinds of spin-offs than those in more isolated locations? To what extent are spin-off rates related to major changes within established organizations? Is success (or lack of success) of the incubator organization related to the performance of spin-off firms?

Environments and relationships

1) How does location in a complex of similar firms bear upon the competitive advantages of new ventures? Do some kinds of new firms benefit more? Do some suffer from being in a complex? How can entrepreneurs limit technology transfer out of their firms when located in a complex?

2) How does location in a complex bear upon the acquisition of informal capital? How does geographic location relate to the practices of institutional investors and lenders?

3) How do entrepreneurs or entrepreneurial teams develop social capital, that is network relationships with others who can assist them? What causes this social capital to erode? What kinds of social capital are more or less valuable to entrepreneurs?

Strategies

1) How can new firms, despite limited experience and scale, develop resources which provide a basis for competitive advantage? What bears upon whether these advantages are sustainable?

2) Under what circumstances can new firms compete directly and successfully with larger firms?

3) Environments vary along various dimensions, including their speed of change. How do successful new ventures differ in their strategies and the resource positions they develop in different kinds of environments?

This short list of possible topics is, of course, only a beginning. Entrepreneurship as an academic field is clearly young and in an early stage of development. The large number of universities making commitments to the field and the growing number of young entrepreneurship scholars support the expectation that there will be great increases in the body of knowledge relating to entrepreneurship in the future. The best is yet to be.

3

Entrepreneurship and Small Business: Toward a Program of Research

W. J. Baumol

Entrepreneurship and small business are patently elements of primary importance for the working of the economy. The evidence indicates that they are the leaders in providing the breakthrough innovations that underlie the unprecedented growth rates of the free market economies and, in this, are at the forefront of the economy's performance. Indeed, they are arguably a focal point and critical strategic entities for any promising program of growth enhancement. At the other extreme, they are the one promising refuge for the impoverished and the unemployed, who can turn to start up business as the only available source of income and a possible way out of poverty. Yet neither of these occupy the place it deserves, either in mainstream research or in the university teaching programs. This paradoxical relationship goes further. Among earlier economists the entrepreneur is frequently mentioned and his or her critical role emphasized. Yet the discussion of the subject is most frequently very brief, and consists generally of a listing of the tasks of the entrepreneur – organizing of the firm, risk bearing, etc., with little that aspires to the status of sophisticated theory.[1] A moment though will surely confirm that this gap in the literature is not neglect of a peripheral matter, but a gaping hole in our understanding of the economic mechanism. Surely research is needed to provide what is missing here, opening the way for material ranging from formal theoretical analysis and the gathering of empirical evidence, to provision of the badly needed teaching material.

The obvious questions are clear:

- Just what research is to be undertaken?
- How is it to be carried out?
- What should prospective entrepreneurs be taught, and what written materials are needed to support such a teaching program?

There are no definitive answers to these questions, and any views on these matters must be expressed carefully to avoid the appearance of opposition to alternative approaches. The pages that follow provide a very personal view of some possible answers based on research and writing on these subjects currently undertaken by a number of colleagues and myself.[2] But first I will offer a few words distinguishing several categories of entrepreneurs for which the pertinent analysis differs, and some comment seeking to indicate the reasons for the gap in our literature, and the implications of these reasons for what one can hope research to accomplish in the arena, approaches that seem promising for the purpose, and recognition of the limiting handicaps that will not be easy to overcome.

---

[1] There are, of course, exceptions, notably in the groundbreaking work of Joseph Schumpeter and Israel Kirzner. I, too, have attempted to provide some analytic contributions to the subject.

[2] The work is conducted under the generous sponsorship of the Ewing Marion Kauffman Foundation. The colleagues involved in these projects include (in alphabetical order) Sue-Anne Blackman, Janeece Lewis, David Landes, Robert Litan, Melissa Schilling, Carl Schram, Robert Strom, and Edward Wolff.

3.1 Three Entrepreneurial Categories

Before getting to the source of the difficulties for creation of such things as a full-scale and operational theory of entrepreneurship it is useful to recognize that they are divisible into three groups that can be labeled (i) innovative entrepreneurs, (ii) replicative entrepreneurs, and (iii) necessity entrepreneurs. This subdivision is helpful because these three groups differ essentially in the motivation underlying their occupational choice and in the nature and magnitude of their contribution to society. My own work is focused on entrepreneurs of the first type because of their crucial role in the growth performance of the economy. I will therefore content myself with a few remarks on the other two categories before turning to the central substance of my discussion.

By replicative entrepreneurs I mean those ambitious individuals who, though they have a choice of occupations, voluntarily select the creation, organization, and direction of a new enterprise of more or less standard variety, as their income-earning activity. The necessity entrepreneurs, in contrast, even though they too found a small enterprise replicating many other firms already in existence (another grocery or tailor shop) they are driven to do so because they have no other choice, they can find no other remunerative occupation that is even minimally acceptable. The innovative entrepreneurs, of course, are those who found a new business that is devoted to the production and dissemination of a new product or process. They may themselves be the inventors, but in the role of entrepreneur their task is the development of the invention to the point where they can bring it to market.

Now, there are several rather surprising facts about the replicative entrepreneurs. First, the preliminary evidence indicates that an increase in their numbers has little or no correlation with at least the current rate of growth of their economy. An economy with a large amount of firm creation activity seems generally to have virtually no advantage in terms of growth rate (see Reynolds *et al.*, 2003, pp. 19–22). Presumably this is because the creation of additional tailor shops or groceries is not critical for expansion of an economy. Second, the evidence shows that those who are self-employed earn less and work longer hours than employed individuals who are otherwise similar (Frey and Benz, 2003, p. 3, Hamilton, 2000).

In surprising contrast to the self-selected replicative entrepreneurs, there is a reported positive correlation of high statistical significance between number of necessity entrepreneurs in an economy and its rate of growth, particularly in a 2- and 3-year lagged relationship (Reynolds *et al.*, 2003, *loc. cit.*). But that is plausibly interpreted as a case of reverse correlation, with growth expanding the number of those self-employed out of necessity, rather than the reverse. The explanation, rather, is that rapid growth cuts jobs to the extent that it entails increased efficiency, and because of changing technology, makes many workers obsolete. The main contribution of this group, it would appear, is not to growth of the economy, but to prevention of destitution and emergence from poverty of the individuals who are heavily in need economically.

It is evidently to the innovative entrepreneurs that we must look for stimulation of growth of the overall economy. And here, too, there is at least preliminary evidence, not just conjecture. Independent entrepreneurs, including luminaries such as Boulton and Watt, Edison, the Wright Brothers and Bill Gates, have been responsible for the preponderance of the more sensational technical breakthroughs that underlie the explosive growth of our economy. Without the work of these entrepreneurs and others our economy's progress since the 17th century might have been distinctly modest.

3.2   What Impedes Entrepreneurship Teaching and Research?

So, given its patent importance, why is the content of a program for instruction of future entrepreneurs so unsettled, and why is the entrepreneur the invisible man of the economic models? One of the problems for teaching entrepreneurship, paradoxically, is that it is too easy. It does not take much education to be an itinerant peddler. But even some innovative entrepreneurs who were spectacularly successful had received minimal education, Edison and the Wright brothers being outstanding examples. Indeed, the hard question is, "what is there to teach an entrepreneur?"

The learning needed by replicative entrepreneurs is often no more that the elementary practicalities of operating a small firm, including bookkeeping and rudimentary knowledge of the pertinent laws such as tax and employee and product safety requirements. In contrast, innovative entrepreneurship is difficult to teach for quite another reason – because, by its definition, an innovation is something different from everything else. What teaching is best qualified to pass on is a repeatable *generality*, such as a widely applicable method of mathematical analysis, or an attribute common to many phenomena. But, by definition and in substance, the critical attributes of any innovation are those features that are *not* common with those of anything else. Innovation is the ultimate in heterogeneous products.

That is a major obstacle to its teaching. But it is also a primary handicap for analysis. The analytic approach typically seeks to point out generalities that were previously unrecognized: the speed of a falling object or the short-run effects of a rise in savings rate on gross domestic product (GDP). But as just noted, a generalization is apt to miss the point when dealing with innovative entrepreneurship. Creativity is difficult to codify.

3.3 What *Can* Research on Entrepreneurship Hope to Discover?

Yet there are generalities that apply, not in description of the activities of innovative entrepreneurs *per se*, but things such as the incentives that drive their efforts and steps that can encourage and facilitate those activities. For example, Schumpeter's groundbreaking analysis described the market mechanism that brings temporary monopoly profits the innovator but rapidly erodes them, so that they *must* soon innovate again if they want to continue earning profits. The present author has stressed the foreclosure of rent-seeking opportunities as the way to direct entrepreneurial activities into productive channels. Such observations can be important for practice as well as for theory, because they indicate what can be done to encourage this critically beneficial activity.

They also suggest promising directions for research on the subject. An illustration is the issue of education of entrepreneurs. As the technology of inventions has grown increasingly complex the technical knowledge needed by the innovating entrepreneur has also grown. But this does not eliminate the need for imagination and creativity, and that raises the question, what educational approaches promote rigorous technical knowledge without at the same time hampering heterodox thinking?

3.4   What Is the Prospective Entrepreneur to Be Taught?

This discussion indicates that useful education of the entrepreneur can proceed at two levels. The one entails the practicalities of organization and operation of a new firm, a subject whose contents are clear. The second imparts more technical knowledge but does so while encouraging creativity rather than slight forward movement along partially well-explored paths. And research on how to do this is surely a promising direction for the interests of society.

But observation on the history of entrepreneurial education suggests some rather disturbing hypotheses. A review of the biographies of the most celebrated of these innovators shows, in a surprising share of these cases, a most remarkable absence of rigorous technical training and, in many cases, little education at all. The obvious names of yore – Watt, Whitney, Fulton, Morse, Edison, and the Wright brothers – illustrate the point.[3]

The preceding observations would seem to lend support to the conjecture that education, in its standard forms, contributes little and may even be a hindrance to technical progress. The current research, already mentioned, being carried out by several colleagues and myself already indicates that this is not inconsistent with the facts. Yet, at the same time, rigorous education does clearly play a critical role in support of technical progress.

---

[3] Samuel Morse did attend Yale but, like Fulton, was trained as an artist. More recently, the jet airplane engine was invented by Frank Whittle, who came up with the idea while he was a pilot in the Royal Air Force, years before he attended Cambridge University.

Historical evidence indicates that the design of the educational process has significant consequences for two highly pertinent, but very different, capabilities of the individuals engaged in innovative activities. On one side, education provides technical competence and mastery of currently available analytic tools to future entrepreneurs and others who will participate in activities related to innovation and growth. On the other side, education can stimulate creativity and imagination, and facilitate their utilization. But it is at least a tenable hypothesis that educational methods that are effective in providing one of these benefits may actually tend to be an obstacle to attainment of the other. For example, the student who has mastered a large body of the received mathematical literature, including theorems, proofs, and methods of calculation, may be led to think in conventional ways that can be an obstacle to unorthodox approaches that favor creativity. And our preliminary evidence suggests that there is a comparable difference between the ways of thinking of the personnel of large industrial laboratories who focus on successive, incremental technical advances in product and process design, and the innovative entrepreneur (the inventive individuals who are responsible for true technological breakthroughs). This suggests that education designed for technical competence and mastery of the available body of analysis and education designed to stimulate originality and heterodox thinking tend to be substitutes more than complements.

How to educate for the two different purposes, then, is surely an appropriate and, indeed, critical subject for future research.

4

The Entrepreneurial Society

D. B. Audretsch

Economics attracted me as a student because it dealt with some of the most pressing issues of the day. The 1970s saw the emergence of a new economic problem; the simultaneous existence of high and persistent unemployment combined with worrisome levels of inflation. The twin threats of unemployment and inflation were so menacing as to warrant a new word – *stagflation*, as well as to provide the two factors underpinning the new *misery index*, which was designed to record the new statistic.

While macroeconomics pondered the impotence of the traditional tried-and-true policy prescriptions to alleviate stagflation, the field of industrial organization suggested a different cause – the large corporation along with its accompanying market power. The short-lived theory of administered pricing argued that the large corporation, such as General Motors or U.S. Steel, enjoyed sufficient size and market dominance that it could elevate prices even as demand was falling.

In fact, the entire field of industrial organization had emerged as a response to a public policy concern over large corporations possessing too much market power as to corrupt the functioning of markets and ultimately the economy. Industrial organization had its roots as a response to the so-called *Trust Problem* emerging in the mid- to late-1800s. The first stirrings of industrial organization as a field came as response to the emergence of the trusts of the late 1900s and their perceived adverse impact on performance criteria such as prices and profits. Not only were the trusts attributed to demolishing family businesses, farms in the Midwest and entire communities, but the public policy debate at the time accused them of threatening the underpinnings of democracy in the United States. In arguing for the passage of the 1890 Act, Senator Sherman argued, "If we will not endure a King as a political power we should not endure a King over the production, transportation, and sale of the necessaries of life. If we would not submit to an emperor we should not submit to an autocrat of trade with power to prevent competition and to fix the price of any commodity."

Later, during the Great Depression, scholars such as Berle and Means (1932) attributed large corporations of possessing sufficient market power as to engage in administered pricing, in that they were able to maintain or even raise prices while demand was falling.

But it was subsequent to the Second World War that the field really took off. When the Premier of the Soviet Union, Nikita Kruschev, banged his table and threatened the then U.S. President John F. Kennedy, "We will bury you," the West was concerned. The policy concern was not restricted to the military threat, but rather included an economic dimension. After all, the Soviet Union, and her former Eastern European satellites were free to enjoy an industry structure that seemed to be incompatible with the democratic traditions to which the West was committed – a complete centralization and concentration of economic activity to within just a single firm in each industry, or what was called the *Kombinate* in East Germany.

Thus, it became the task of the scholars toiling in the field of industrial organization to explicitly identify what exactly was gained and lost as a result of large-scale production and a concentration of economic ownership and decision-making. During the post-war period a generation of scholars galvanized the field of industrial organization by developing a research agenda dedicated to identifying the issues involving this perceived trade-off between economic efficiency on the one hand, and political and economic decentralization on the other. Scholarship in industrial organization generated a massive literature focusing on essentially three issues:

(1) What are the gains to size and large-scale production?
(2) What are the economic welfare implications of having an oligopolistic or concentrated market structure (i.e. Is economic performance promoted or reduced in an industry with just a handful of large-scale firms?)
(3) Given the overwhelming evidence that large-scale production resulting in economic concentration is associated with increased efficiency, what are the public policy implications?

Oliver Williamson's classic 1968 article "Economies as an Antitrust Defense: The Welfare Tradeoffs," published in the *American Economic Review*, became something of a final statement demonstrating what appeared to be an inevitable trade-off between the gains in productive efficiency from increased concentration and gains in terms of competition, and implicitly democracy, from decentralizing policies (Williamson, 1968). But it did not seem possible to have both; certainly not in Williamson's completely static model.

Thus, one of the most fundamental policy issue confronting Western Europe and North America during the post-war era was how to live with this apparent trade-off between economic concentration and productive efficiency on the one hand, and decentralization and democracy on the other. The public policy question of the day was, *How can society reap the benefits of the large corporation in an oligopolistic setting while avoiding or at least minimizing the costs imposed by a concentration of economic power?* The policy response was to constrain the freedom of firms to contract. Such policy restraints typically took the form of public ownership, regulation, and competition policy or antitrust. At the time, considerable attention was devoted to what seemed like glaring differences in policy approaches to this apparent trade-off by different countries. France and Sweden resorted to government owner-ship of private business. Other countries, such as the Netherlands and Germany, tended to emphasize regulation. Still other countries, such as the Untied States, had a greater emphasis on antitrust. In fact, most countries relied on elements of all three policy instruments. While the particular instrument may have varied across countries, they were, in fact, manifestations of a singular policy approach – how to restrict and restrain the power of the large corporation. What may have been per-ceived as a disparate set of policies at the time appears in retrospect to comprise a remarkably singular policy approach.

Western economists and policy-makers of the day were nearly unan-imous in their acclaim for large-scale enterprises. It is no doubt an irony of history that this consensus mirrored a remarkably similar gigantism embedded in Soviet doctrine, fueled by the writings of Marx and ulti-mately implemented by the iron fist of Stalin. This was the era of mass production when economies of scale seemed to be the decisive factor in determining efficiency. This was the world so colorfully described by Galbraith (1956) in his Theory of Countervailing Power, in which big business was held in check by big labor and by big government. This was the era of the man in the gray flannel suit (Riesman, 1950) and the organization man (Whyte, 1960), when virtually every major social and economic institution acted to reinforce the stability and predictability needed for mass production (Poire and Sabel, 1984, Chandler, 1977).

With a decided focus on the role of large corporations, oligopoly, and economic concentration, the literature on industrial organization yielded a number of key insights concerning the efficiency and impact on economic performance associated with new and small firms:

(1) Small firms were generally less efficient than their larger counterparts. Studies from the United States in the 1960s and 1970 revealed that small firms produced at lower levels of efficiency.

(2) Small firms provided lower levels of employee compensa-tion. Empirical evidence from both North America and Europe found a systematic and positive relationship between employee compensation and firm size.

(3) Small firms were only marginally involved in innovative activity. Based on R&D measures, SMEs accounted for only a small amount of innovative activity.

(4) The relative importance of small firms was declining over time in both North America and Europe.

Thus, while a heated debate emerged about which approach best promoted large-scale production while simultaneously constraining the ability of large corporations to exert market power, there was much less debate about public policy toward small business and entrepreneurship. The only issue was whether public policy-makers should simply allow small firms to disappear as a result of their inefficiency or intervene to preserve them on social and political grounds. Those who perceived small firms to contribute significantly to growth, employment generation, and competitiveness were few and far between.

In the post-war era, small firms and entrepreneurship were viewed as a luxury, perhaps needed by the West to ensure a decentralization of decision-making; but obtained only at a cost to efficiency. Certainly the systematic empirical evidence, gathered from both Europe and North America documented a sharp trend toward a decreased role of small firms during the post-war period.

Public policy toward small firms generally reflected the view of economists and other scholars that they were a drag on economic efficiency and growth, generated lower quality jobs in terms of direct and indirect compensation, and were generally on the way to becoming less important to the economy, if not threatened by long-term extinction. Some countries, such as the former Soviet Union, but also Sweden and France, adapted the policy stance of allowing small firms to gradually disappear and account for a smaller share of economic activity.

The public policy stance of the United States reflected long-term political and social valuation of small firms that seemed to reach back to the Jeffersonian traditions of the country. Thus, the public policy toward small business in the United States was oriented toward preserving what was considered to be inefficient enterprises, which, if left unprotected, might otherwise become extinct.

Even advocates of small business agreed that small firms were less efficient than big companies. These advocates were willing to sacrifice a modicum of efficiency, however, because of other contributions – moral, political, and otherwise – made by small business to society. Small business policy was thus "preservationist" in character. For example, the passage of the Robinson–Patman Act in 1936, along with its widespread enforcement in the post-war era, was widely interpreted as one effort to protect small firms, like independent retailers, that would otherwise have been too inefficient to survive in open competition with large corporations. Preservationist policies were clearly at work in the creation of the U.S. Small Business Administration. In the *Small Business Act* of July 10, 1953, Congress authorized the creation of the Small Business Administration, with an explicit mandate to "aid, counsel, assist and protect ... the interests of small business concerns."[1] *The Small Business Act* was clearly an attempt by the Congress to halt the continued disappearance of small businesses and to preserve their role in the U.S. economy.

If physical capital was at the heart of the Solow economy, knowledge capital replaced it in the Romer economy. While the policy goals of economic growth remained relatively unchanged, the Romer model reflected the emergence of a new emphasis on a strikingly different policy mechanism, knowledge capital, involving very different policy instruments (Romer, 1986).

Entrepreneurship and small firms seemed at least as incompatible with the knowledge-based Romer economy as they were in the capital-based Solow economy (Solow, 1956). The most prevalent theory of innovation in economics, the model of the knowledge production function, suggested that knowledge-generating inputs, such as research and development (R&D) were a prerequisite to generating innovative output. With their limited and meager investments in R&D, at least in absolute terms, new and small firms did not seem to possess sufficient knowledge capabilities to be competitive in a knowledge-based economy.

It must not be forgotten that as recently as the first election of Bill Clinton, many scholars and policy-makers looked to Japan and

---

[1] http://www.sba.gov/aboutsba/sbahistory.html

Germany to redirect the flagging U.S. economy. This sentiment generally mirrored the influential study, *Made in America*, directed by the
leaders of the MIT Commission on Industrial Productivity, Michael L.
Dertouzos, Richard K. Lester, and Robert M. Solow. It was a team
of 23 scholars, spanning a broad range of disciplines and backgrounds,
who reached the conclusion that for the United States to restore its
international competitiveness, it had to adapt the types of policies
targeting the leading corporations prevalent in Japan and Germany.
Thurow bemoaned that the United States was "losing the economic
race,"[2] because, "Today it's very hard to find an industrial corporation
in America that isn't in really serious trouble basically because of trade
problems ... The systematic erosion of our competitiveness comes from
having lower rates of growth of manufacturing productivity year after
year, as compared with the rest of the world" (Thurow, 1985, p. 23).
W.W. Restow predicted a revolution in economic policy, concluding
that, "The United States is entering a new political era, one in which
it will be preoccupied by increased economic competition from abroad
and will need better cooperation at home to deal with this challenge."[3]
However, neither Rostow nor Thurow predicted that this new focus of
public policy to restore U.S. growth and competitiveness in globally
linked markets would be on entrepreneurship.

However, in searching for the innovative advantage of different types
of firms, Zoltan Acs and I (1988, 1990) surprisingly found that small firms
provided the engines of innovative activity, at least in certain industries.
The breakdown of the model of the knowledge production function at the
level of the firm raises the question, *Where do innovative firms with little or no R&D get the knowledge inputs?* This question becomes particularly relevant for small and new firms that undertake little R&D themselves, yet contribute considerable innovative activity in newly emerging
industries such as biotechnology and computer software. One clue sup-
plied by the literature on the new economic geography identifying the
local nature of knowledge spillovers is from other, third-party firms or

---

[2] L. Thurow, "Losing the economic race," *New York Review of Books*, pp. 29–31, September
1984.

[3] W. W. Restow, "Here comes a new political chapter in America," *International Herald
Tribune*, vol. 2, January 1987.

research institutions, such as universities, that may be located within spatial proximity (Audretsch, 1995). Economic knowledge may spill over from the firm conducting the R&D or the research laboratory of a university for access by a new and small firm.

How can new and small firms access such knowledge spillovers? And why should new and small firms have a competitive advantage accessing knowledge produce elsewhere vis-à-vis their larger counterparts? That is, what are the mechanisms transmitting the spillover of knowledge from the source producing that knowledge, such as the R&D laboratory of a large corporation, or a university, to the small firm actually engaged in commercializing that knowledge.

The discrepancy in organizational context between the organization creating opportunities and those exploiting the opportunities that seemingly contradicted the model of the firm knowledge production function was resolved in my 1995 book by introducing the Knowledge Spillover Theory of Entrepreneurship, "The findings challenge an assumption implicit to the knowledge production function – that firms exist exogenously and then endogenously seek out and apply knowledge inputs to generate innovative output.... It is the knowledge in the possession of economic agents that is exogenous, and in an effort to appropriate the returns from that knowledge, the spillover of knowledge from its producing entity involves endogenously creating a new firm" (Audretsch, 1995, pp. 179–180).

What is the source of this entrepreneurial opportunity that endogenously generated the startup of new firms? The answer seemed to be through the spillover of knowledge that created the opportunities for the startup of a new firm, "How are these small and frequently new firms able to generate innovative output when undertaken a generally negligible amount of investment into knowledge-generating inputs, such as R&D? One answer is apparently through exploiting knowledge created by expenditures on research in universities and on R&D in large corporations" (Audretsch, 1995, p. 179).

The empirical evidence supporting the knowledge spillover theory of entrepreneurship was provided by analyzing variations in startup rates across various industries reflecting different underlying knowledge contexts. In particular, those industries with a greater investment in new knowledge also exhibited higher startup rates while those industries with less investment in new knowledge exhibited lower startup rates, which was interpreted as a conduit transmitting knowledge spillovers.

Thus, compelling evidence was provided suggesting that entrepreneurship is an endogenous response to opportunities created but not exploited by the incumbent firms. This involved an organizational dimension involving the mechanism transmitting knowledge spillovers – the startup of new firms. Additionally, Jaffe (1989), Audretsch and Feldman (1996) and Audretsch and Stephan (1996) provided evidence concerning the spatial dimension of knowledge spillovers. In particular, their findings suggested that knowledge spillovers are geographically bounded and localized within spatial proximity to the knowledge source. None of these studies, however, identified the actual mechanisms which actually transmit the knowledge spillover; rather, the spillovers were implicitly assumed to automatically exist (or fall like Manna from heaven), but only within a geographically bounded spatial area.

The knowledge spillover theory of entrepreneurship contests the view that entrepreneurial opportunities are exogenous and only individual-specific characteristics and attributes influence the cognitive process underlying the entrepreneurial decision to start a firm. Rather, the knowledge spillover theory of entrepreneurship explicitly identifies an important source of opportunities – investments in knowledge and ideas made by firms and universities that are not completely commercialized. By linking the degree of entrepreneurial activity to the degree of knowledge investments in a *Standort*, systematic empirical evidence was provided suggesting that entrepreneurial opportunities are not at all exogenous, but rather endogenous to the extent of investments in new knowledge. In a comprehensive study with colleagues at the Max Planck Institute, we found that regions rich in knowledge generated a greater amount of entrepreneurial opportunities than regions with impoverished knowledge (Audretsch et al., 2005). This empirical evidence confirmed the theory suggesting that entrepreneurial opportunities are not exogenous to the context but, rather, systematically related to the knowledge context.

The knowledge spillover theory of entrepreneurship identified one such mechanism by which knowledge created with one context and purpose spills over from the organization creating it to the organization actually attempting to commercialize that knowledge. Entrepreneurship has emerged as a vital organizational form for economic growth because it provides the missing link (Acs *et al.*, 2004) in the process of economic growth. By serving as a conduit for the spillover of knowledge, entrepreneurship is a mechanism by which investments, both private and public, generate a greater social return, in terms of economic growth and job creation.

Audretsch *et al.* (2005) suggest that in addition to labor, physical capital, and knowledge capital, the endowment of entrepreneurship capital also matters for generating economic growth. Entrepreneurship capital refers to the capacity for the *Standort*, that is, the geographically relevant spatial units of observation to generate the startup of new enterprises.

The concept of *social capital* (Putnam, 1993, Coleman, 1988) added a social component to the traditional factors shaping economic growth and prosperity. Together with Max Keilbach and Erik Lehmann at the Max Planck Institute (Audretsch *et al.*, 2005), we suggest that what has been called social capital in the entrepreneurship literature may actually be a more specific sub-component, which they introduce as *entrepreneurship capital*. The entrepreneurship capital of an economy or a society refers to the institutions, culture, and historical context that is conducive to the creation of new firms. This involves a number of aspects such as social acceptance of entrepreneurial behavior but of course also individuals who are willing to deal with the risk of creating new firms and the activity of bankers and venture capital agents that are willing to share risks and benefits involved. Hence entrepreneurship capital reflects a number of different legal, institutional and social factors and forces. Taken together, these factors and forces constitute the entrepreneurship capital of an economy, which creates a capacity for entrepreneurial activity.

By including measures of entrepreneurship capital along with the traditional factors of physical capital, knowledge capital, and labor in a production function model estimating economic growth, we found pervasive and compelling econometric evidence suggesting that entrepreneurship capital also contributes to economic growth (Audretsch *et al.*, 2005).

Public policy did not wait for the painstaking econometric evidence linking entrepreneurship to economic growth. The mandate for entrepreneurship policy has generally emerged from what would superficially appear to be two opposite directions. One direction emanates from the failure of the traditional policy instruments, corresponding to the Solow model, or those based on instruments promoting investment into physical capital, to adequately maintain economic growth and employment in globally linked markets. The emergence of entrepreneurship policy as a *bona fide* approach to generating economic growth and job creation has been rampant through the old rust belt of the industrial Midwest in the United States, ranging from cities such as Cleveland and Pittsburg to states such as Wisconsin and Indiana who are pinning their economic development strategies on entrepreneurship policies.

The second push for the entrepreneurship policy mandate is from the opposite direction – the failure of the so-called new economy policy instruments, corresponding to the Romer model, or those promoting investment into knowledge capital to adequately generate economic growth and employment. Recognition of the *European Paradox*, where employment creation and economic growth remain meager, despite world-class levels of human capital and research capabilities triggered the Lisabon Proclomation stating that Europe would become the entrepreneurship leader by 2020.

Although coming from opposite directions, both have in common an unacceptable economic performance. In other words, the mandate for entrepreneurship policy is rooted in dissatisfaction – dissatisfaction with the *status quo*, and in particular, with the *status quo* economic performance.[4]

As the initial capital-driven Solow model and the more recent knowledge-driven Romer model have not delivered the expected levels

---

[4] A third direction contributing to the mandate for entrepreneurship policy may be in the context of less developed regions and developing countries. Such regions have had endowments of neither physical capital nor knowledge capital but still look to entrepreneurship capital to serve as an engine of economic growth.

of economic performance by themselves, a mandate for entrepreneurship policy has emerged and begun to diffuse throughout the entire globe. Whether or not specific policy instruments will work in their particular contexts is not the point of this paper. What is striking, however, is the emergence and diffusion of an entirely new public policy approach to generate economic growth – the creation of the entrepreneurial society. It is upon this new mantel of the entrepreneurial society that *Standorte*, ranging from communities to cities, states and even entire nations, hang their hopes, dreams, and aspirations for prosperity and security.

5

What to Make of the Changes in Industrial Districts? Three Questions

C. Sabel

Here are terse characterizations or three, closely changes manifestly underway in industrial districts, and the questions they raise. I take it to be almost self-evident, among experts, that something like the changes described are indeed taking place, and that no one knows precisely what to make of them here.

Industrial districts are on the move. Recent studies have found that lead firms in key districts are "delocalizing" production of key components, and outsourcing various steps in the manufacturing process to non-district firms, typically abroad. Many of these same firms are formalizing competition for their business among local subcontractors. Even as they reorganize their supply chains, these firms are concentrating more on knowledge-intensive activities such as design and the research and development associated with it. Much of this activity is still located in the firms' home district; but it, too, is

increasingly organized through long-distance networks linking design-
ers and researchers at distant sites (often themselves located in widely
separated districts) through sophisticated new communications technologies. All these changes go hand in hand with a shift toward less
personal or family-based forms of corporate governance. Whereas a
decade ago it seemed (mistakenly) that the districts were being invaded
by multinational firms or subverted from within by the tentacular, local
expansion of their own lead firms, today, more probably for better than
for worse, the district as an entity is in some elusive sense in motion.

But what are we to make of the new relations within and among
firms locally and at long distance? Do they, for example, reflect (and
advance) an increasing modularization of production, so that catalogs
of specification can somehow replace more context specific, if not per-
sonally intimate forms of collaboration? Do they on the contrary reflect
the dramatic decrease in communication and other transaction costs,
where opportunism is disciplined by the actors' understanding that
they are engaged in, and stand to benefit hugely from continuing with,
repeat play? Or (as I myself am inclined to believe) do the new relations
reflection deep, "pragmatist" organizational changes that allow firms
to use the same continuous flow of information that must be exchanged
to co-design products that no one can specify *ex ante* to monitor their
partners' probity as well? (For current discussion of these possibilities,
see Charles F. Sabel and Jonathan Zeitlin, "Neither Modularity Nor
Relational Contracting: Inter-Firm Collaboration in the New Economy.
A Critique of Langlois and Lamoreaux, Raff, and Temin," *Enterprise
and Society* vol. 5, no. 3 (September 2004, with further references.)

Until roughly the early 1990s districts were thought to be largely
self-governing. Or, more exactly, their ability spontaneously to provide
themselves the governance apparatus they needed was part – an indis-
pensable part – of what made them districts in the first place. Thus
there was in the districts an "obvious" need for standard "real" services:
quality assurance, technology scanning, payroll, accounting, and other
functions required by firms that were too small to serve themselves.
It was equally obvious which regional institutions and sectoral associations were "naturally" positioned to provide them, and even which
kinds of leftist and center-right political cultures were the "natural"

seedbeds of the propitious kind of associationalism. Because the typical district governance institutions were rooted in associations, the associations in political cultures, and the political cultures in forms of sociability, it was easy (though historically inaccurate, and egregiously so) to see the districts as organic growths, inseparable from their place of origin, but requiring no deliberate cultivation precisely because of their natural affinity for it.

But for at least the last decade neither the needs nor the relevant actors have been anything like self-evident. On the contrary: many of the older generation of institutions providing real services have been closed, and disagreements over possible successors have hampered the development of new ones. The associations out of which those institutions grew are in a constant state of re-organization, searching for new tasks for members with increasingly sophisticated and individual needs. The political subcultures that housed the associations are of course in turmoil, most obviously because the parties, the party system, and the ideological divisions on which the party system was founded have been changed almost beyond recognition. As a result, the process for deciding how to choose new infrastructures has become a matter of intense local debate, with different regions and districts choosing different procedures, none of them "natural."

Is this intense debate the expression of a transitional period of adjustment, during which the traditional associations will reconfigure themselves so as to be able to address the new tasks? Or, assuming that the restructuring in the districts in the result of drift toward a world of modules or (transaction) costless repeat play, will the district firms of the new future become self-governing enough to dispense with any like an exoskeleton of district institutions? Or, assuming that the restructuring in the districts grows from a shift in the direction of "pragmatist" firm organization, do firms of this novel kind need an district infrastructure, and how might the services provided, and the manner of their provision, reflect distinctive features of "pragmatist" response to a highly volatile environment and the need to regularly examine the sustainability of current routines?

Districts are now a developing country phenomenon (almost) as much a fact of economic life in the rich countries. In some cases the developing world districts are new – the direct offshoot of the restructuring described above – and their capacity for autonomous action is, for the moment, limited. But in more established cases, developing country districts threaten to displace rich-country leaders. Brazilian leather shoes and Chinese ceramic tiles are only two prominent examples. Success in such cases owes a good deal to collaboration with capital goods suppliers from, or related to, developed country districts; and this connection is often regarded as something close to treachery by the machine makers' traditional, home country customers. But treasonous or not, the relations between advanced country capital-goods suppliers and emerging districts will only be strengthened in the coming years – unless, of course, the new districts find or help nurture the development of capital-goods suppliers in their own, rapidly growing domestic markets.

How, if at all, are the developing world districts governed? What is the relation of their governance systems, to the extent they have one, to the traditional or emergent governance systems of the rich-country districts? What are the possibilities, if any, for the (mutually transformative) co-governance of related developing and developed-country districts?

Better characterizations of the changes, more trenchant formulation of the open questions, and – above all – answers to the puzzles that change thrusts upon us are all very, very welcome. I look forward to the discussion.

6

Some Notes on the Empirical Basis of the Role Attributed to Small Business and Entrepreneurship in the Thought of Alfred Marshall

G. Becattini

6.1 On Marshall's Industrial Field Work

When Marshall shifted his intellectual interests from philosophy and psychology to economics, besides his excellent – for his times – mathematical preparation, he had already got some general ideas on society and the method proper to the study of social subjects.[1] Among the earliest economic readings of a young mathematician there was, understandably, Cournot's book,[2] that he appreciated very much, except for what Marshall called the "Cournot problem" that is of reconciling

---

[1] See, Whitaker (1975), Becattini (1975), Dardi (1984), Groenewegen (1995), Whitaker (1996), and Raffaelli (2003).

[2] Cournot (1938).

competitive equilibrium with increasing returns. Marshall realized that according to the Cournotian conclusions, the Smithian invisible hand would be frustrated by a tendency of the structure of the competitive markets to become a mosaic of monopolies.

As he wrote to Flux in 1898:

> *One of the chief purposes of my* Wander-jahre *among factories, etc., was to discover how Cournot's premises were wrong.*[3]

This *Wander-jahre*, Marshall tells us, spanned several years:

> *In the years of my apprenticeship to economic studies, between 1867 and 1875, I endeavoured to learn enough of the methods of operation of the greater part of the leading industries of the country (...) This endeavour was associated with an attempt to form a rough estimate of the faculties and training needed for working each (part of machines used), and the strain involved therein: and my guide – if as generally happened he was the employer or a foreman – would generally answer my inquires as to the wages which each was receiving.*[4]

While the relationships between Marshall and classical and marginalist economic thought has been deeply explored, Marshall's field work has practically received no attention. This is due – partially, at least – to the fact that very few documents of such activity survive. Another cause of such neglect is the widespread belief that it was made in a rather amateurish way, giving rise to some of the most disputable concepts enunciated by Marshall (e.g. life cycle of the firm, representative firm, etc.).

Nevertheless, some writings of the period 1873–1874, some letters to his mother from America in 1875, some pages of *What I Remember* by Mary Paley Marshall, his testimonial to the Commission for

---

[3] Cfr. (Whitaker, 1975, vol. 3, pp. 227–228)
[4] Pigou (1925, p. 358).

the 1891 Census, other documents[5] and, finally, some autobiographical memories, can give us the scent – at least – of such an activity. In the year 1873 Marshall gave some *Lectures to Women*,[6] discussing the main industrial relations issues of the time. Thanks to an attentive reading of the "Blue Books", some contacts with trade unionist (e.g. T. Burt, J. Holmes[7]), and with some friends of the Trade Unions (e.g. J.M. Ludlow), Marshall came to know a lot about the working conditions in several British industries of his time. This interest in labor conditions was not merely due to philanthropy, but also – and perhaps even to a greater extent – to the conviction that, throughout its influence on the character of the worker, the organization of labor within the factory influences the rate of increase of labor productivity, which forms the basis of the progress of the competitiveness of the country, as well as of the well-being of its inhabitants.

Marshall started his career as an economist so convinced that the industrial relations of a country have a decisive impact on its competitiveness as to advise his pupil Foxwell: *Firmness of grasp and practical acquaintance with the social relations of industry seem to be the main requirements from the lecturer.*[8]

The letters to his mother from the United States illustrate another aspect of Marshall's interest in industrial phenomenology. We give the list, probably partial, of the visits he paid to American factories: *Large stove works; large reaping and moving machine works; large Bessemer works; horse shoe works; huge cotton mills; Mason and Hamlins, Organ Factory; Pacific Cotton Mills; Lowell Manufacturing Works (Carpets); Chikering Piano Works; Virginia Consolidated Mines; American Glass Manufacture.*[9] Notwithstanding its crudity, this list of visited factories can give us an idea of the wideness and variety of the interests of the young Marshall. Wideness and variety that probably reflect a host of visits previously paid to British factories, since the theme

---

[5] See, e.g. the two volumes of *Official Papers* edited by Keynes (1926) and Groenewegen (1996).
[6] Raffaelli *et al.* (1995).
[7] *Ibid.*, pp. 176–194.
[8] Whitaker (1975, vol. I, p. 28,).
[9] Whitaker (1975, vol. I, pp. 49–82).

which dominates the letters is a comparison between American and British manufacture. We should also notice that several letters include designs representing processes or implements considered important and/or new.

Further evidence of his attention to industrial phenomena – this time relative to the eighties – comes from Mary Paley Marshall's delightful *What I Remember*.[10] *In vacations, either at home or abroad, we spent some time in towns, seeing factories and workshops. One year we would go to the pottery district with its problems of localisation of industry and changing fashions (...) Another year it would be the light metal trades (...) I remember specially the file-making industry of Sheffield where machinery was just beginning to displace manual labour.* Mary meaningfully adds that *Alfred knew all about machines and tools ... He could tell beforehand what wages were being paid for any kind of work and was seldom wrong by more than a few pence a week.*

And finally, a very interesting notation, characteristic of one peculiar aspect of the Marshallian approach to industrial phenomena: *We used to stand at the gates of factories when work stopped to watch the workers coming out.*[11]

If we put all these little pieces of information together, we come to the conclusion – we believe – that the young Marshall strove to deepen his knowledge of the economic, technological and organizational aspects of British industry, but always – we must notice – in the framework of the socio-cultural conditions of the manufacturing communities.

6.2   Marshall and British Industrial Statistics

There has been much argument concerning the Marshallian methodological practice of field research, with many critics dubbing it as not properly scientific, but rather "impressionist".[12]

---

[10] Marshall (1947)

[11] *Ibid.*, pp. 42–43.

[12] Marshall himself, higly praising *Lancashire Cotton Industry* by S. Chapman, defined it: *both a realistic-impressionist study of human life, and an economic treatise.* Whitaker (1975, vol. III, p. 93).

Some authors see in it a sort of retrogressive attitude when compared to the contemporary advance of statistical thought. For example, Marshall's (negative) influence on the faithful Edgeworth (perhaps the strongest statistical theoretician of his time) has been charged with the scarcity of statistically sophisticated papers in the first decades of the *Economic Journal*.[13]

The truth is perhaps different: Marshall was certainly convinced of the great importance of statistical data for economic analysis, but had a very low opinion of the quality of the British industrial statistics.[14]

It is due – we guess – to this low opinion of British statistical data that he preferred Le Play's method of *an intensive study of all the details of the domestic life of a few carefully selected families* (in his case firms) to the prevailing one of *the extensive method of first rapidly collecting a large number of observations with the hope that any inexactitudes and oddities will balance each other out, and subsequently proceeding to interpret the data in the form of statistics.* The first of these two methods – he adds – requires a *"rare combination of painstaking care in selecting the cases and acute perception and sympathy in interpreting them, is – at its best – the best of them all"*. But, he acutely concludes: *in ordinary hands it is likely to suggest less reliable conclusions than the other.*[15]

In this reading of Marshall's thought, his reluctance to apply sophisticated statistical tools appears to be based on his, already mentioned, low opinion of British industrial statistics and to his distrust in an appropriate, short-term, improvement of them.

The point I want to make here is that some far-reaching theoretical changes Marshall introduced already in his (and Mary's) early *Economics of Industry* were based on his intensive, direct, exploration of British manufactures, no less than on a critical examination of both classical and post-classical economic literature.

---

[13] See Jha (1973).

[14] See Marshall testimonial in: Report of the Committee appointed to inquire into the Census, London: *Parliamentary Papers 1890* [Cmnd 6071], LVIII. Minutes of Evidence 1462–1565).

[15] See Marshall (1961, vol. I, p. 97, no. 1).

6.3 Small Business and Industrial Districts

When Marshall published (1st ed., 1879) his little book, the industrial districts phenomenon had already attracted the attention of many observers.[16] Nevertheless the ideas prevailing in the most popular political economy manuals of the time (e.g. J. S. Mill, J. E. Cairnes, and H. Fawcett) did not much help its correct interpretation.

On the way of such full understanding there were some obstacles. The two idols of contemporary economists, the "factory system" and the obsession for "large-scale economies", attributed a mere residual and transitory role to small firms, and consequently to the aggregates of small factories located in the industrial districts of the Midlands.

With the introduction of two new concepts – the economies external to the single factory but internal to groups of factories and the "industrial atmosphere" of the manufacturing communities – the situation changed. As a matter of fact, Marshall combined them to forge the idea, not of a mere territorial concentration of factories but rather of a true "industrial community".

The starting point of the Marshall's reasoning was: *The manufacture of a commodity often consists of several distinct stages, to each of which a separate room in the factory is devoted. But if the total amount of the commodity produced is very large, it may be profitable to devote separate small factories to each of these steps.*[17] However:*Small factories, whatever their number, will be at a great disadvantage relatively to large unless many of them are collected together in the same district.*[18]

The grouping of them in a certain district can have several effects; it can produce:

(a) an "industrial atmosphere" that permeates the entire community in which the group of firms are embedded, where *if one man starts a new idea, it is taken up by others and combined with suggestions of their own; and thus it becomes the source of further new ideas*;

---

[16] See e.g. Cooke (1841), Sargant (1857) and Hearn (1863).
[17] Marshall and M. P. (1879, p. 52).
[18] *Ibid.*, p. 53.

   (b) a specialized labour market: *Employers are apt to resort to any place where they are likely to find a good choice of workers with the special skill which they require; while men seeking employment naturally go to places where there are many employers who need such skill as theirs;*

   (c) a climate of trust and loyalty among the members, employers, and employed, of the industrial community which represents a true "social capital" of the place;[19]

   (d) a multiplicity of *subsidiary industries to meet the special wants of the original population of small factories* (e.g. specialized machinery);

   (e) a sense of belonging to the producing community, *social forces* – Marshall concludes – *here cooperate with economic.*[20]

Thus both large and small factories are benefited (. . .) But these benefits are most important to the small factories, and free them from many of the disadvantages under which they would otherwise labour in competition with large factories.[21]

Marshall defines the industrial district in such a way as to make it an efficient alternative to the vertically integrated factory belonging to a big firm. The subject is very complex, and we are not going into it here; we limit ourselves to point out that with his theory of the industrial district. Marshall demonstrates that there are conditions of organization of production (and common life) in which even a small factory can be efficient, and the corresponding firm competitive.

Apart from the industrial district theme, the issue of small firms receives more attention in the thought of Marshall, but we are not going into it, here. We add only that, generally speaking, Marshall considered them the best nurseries of creativity in business[22] even in what we now call the Fordist Age of Capitalism.

Concluding, for a wide number of commodities (i.e. differentiated and personalized), and at certain, not infrequent, socio-cultural condi-

---

[19] A. Marshall adds: *there are often strong friendships between employers and employed*, Marshall (1961, vol. I, p. 272).

[20] Marshall (1961, vol. I, p. 271).

[21] Marshal and M. P. (1879, p. 47).

[22] See Marshall (1919, pp. 249, 525).

tions, small firms can be efficient and competitive against bigger and more structured firms.

Had this conclusion been adopted in 19th century by the generality of the economists, we would have had, since then, a two-ways-to-industrialization background to development studies, instead of the "one best way" we had.

All that has been said so far is only valid for a world similar to the world Marshall studied in his youth, in which each firm incorporates, so to speak, a "project of life", and its selling or buying is exceptional. But *when the policy of any particular establishment is likely to be governed, not with a single eye to its own success, but in subordination to some large stock-exchange manoeuvre, or some campaign for the control of markets,*[23] we plunge into a different world.

6.4   Entrepreneurship

We cannot certainly say that Marshall introduced the concept of the entrepreneur into economic discourse. From Cantillon onward, at least, the concept was latent, if not explicit, in many economic writings. But the structure of the classic theory of value represented a big obstacle to its accueil, because the triggerer of economic activity was considered to be the capitalist trying to make the most of his capital.

The development of a nationwide banking system gradually changed the situation. During the intermediate decades of the century it became possible for a pushing man, with ideas and a sound reputation, to obtain the capital necessary to start a firm. Marshall explores the British industry in this period and comes to the conclusion that *it is no more true that a man becomes an employer because he is a capitalist. Men command capital because they have the qualifications to profitably employ labour.*[24] To this far-reaching statement Marshall adds the definition of entrepreneurship as a very peculiar kind of skilled work. The required skill consists mainly of: (a) the capacity to go straight to the kernel of the practical problems, (b) to see almost instinctively

---

[23] Marshall (1961, vol. I, p. XII).
[24] Marshall and M. P. (1879, p. 118).

the relative proportions of things, (c) to be a leader of men.[25] This representation of the capitalist-entrepreneur completes the theoretical *bouleversement* and opens the way to the neoclassical theory of distribution.

Marshall has been charged with an apologetic intent, and nobody can exclude that a reaction to some potentially revolutionary implications of the classical theory of distribution acted upon him, but we want to underline that the industrial phenomena of the period make his position quite understandable. More explicitly, we mean that it is plausible to see a sort of convergence of a certain line of thought (Smith, Senior, Mill), with an original attempt to conceptualize what was really happening – or better, Marshall believed was happening.

The young Marshall, of course, did not approach industrial phenomena of his time virgin of any theory, nor without specific hypothesis to verify (e.g. Cournot's problem); nonetheless, our opinion is that he was strongly imbued by the idea of making political economy more "realistic". This theme of the "realism" of political economy recurs much in his correspondence, and we believe it was a sincere reaction to the empty dogmatism of many Ricardo's epigones.

What is sure – we believe – is that his visits to manufactures in the Midlands, giving him the opportunity to exchange views with undertakers, that were, or depicted themselves, as self-made men, influenced his ideas no less than his ruminations on previous economic thought.

We should not forget that after 1850–1860 British manufacturing entered a period of vertical dis-integration and specialization that by itself reduced the average size of the firms in several industries and increased the number of undertakers. This tendency to vertical dis-integration, far from being a negative phenomenon, was the base of a finer distribution of productive functions. The example of the separation of weaving from spinning in textile – both cotton and wool – industry speaks for itself.[26] This process made it possible the entry to the host of new men scarcely provided with capital, but with a good

---

[25] A. Marshall (1961, vol. I, p. 606).
[26] Cfr. Church (1980).

reputation as regards their honesty and technical capacity. It is the period when the books of Samuel Smiles, such as *Character* and *Self-help*, were best-sellers.

6.5   The Italian Revival of Some Marshallian Themes

The students of Italian industrial development after the Second World War came to understand Marshall's interpretation of the industrialization process only after a long intellectual struggle.[27] In fact, the dominant economic theories, Neoclassic or Marxist, conceived the process of dis-integration of Italian manufacturing, that followed the so-called "Italian Miracle" (1951–1963), mainly, or only, as a fragmentation of the biggest firms under the challenge of strong leftist unions. Without noticing the territorial distribution of the phenomena, the majority of the scholars and of the politicians held negative opinions on the proliferation of a crowd of mainly small, sometimes very small, manufacturing firms.

The true meaning of the phenomenon became clear only after the acquisition of the basic principles of the Marshallian theory of industrial districts.[28] The proliferation of small firms then came to be considered not the mere effect of the decisions of the biggest firms but the effect of a combination of causes: (a) the increase of per capita average income, (b) the incipient saturation of the demand for standardized consumption goods; (c) the will to escape the factory dependency of the most enterprising among the skilled workers; and (d) the tendency of big firms to split processes and decentralize certain phases of production.

Well, one the protagonists of this saga, certainly not the only, but perhaps the crucial one, was the small Marshallian entrepreneur.

Two aspects of the problem need clarification: on the one hand, we must underline the socially and historically rooted conditions of such a crop. Many new entries came from inside the industry (e.g. specialized workers, technicians, white collars, etc.), but a consistent number of them came also from outside the industrial world (e.g. ex-shoppers, ex-sharecroppers, etc.). It must be added that large part of

---

[27] See Becattini and Musotti.
[28] See Pyke *et al.* (1990).

Italy benefited from a generation of honest and efficient local administrators of low social extraction (e.g. blue collars and sharecroppers), frequently of left wing ideas. The constructive dialectics between these two classes of newcomers, small entrepreneurs and local administrators, is at the roots of the Italian phenomenon of industrial districts.[29] Despite, we repeat, the insensitivity of all the political parties and of large part of the economic academia.

In conclusion, the nucleus of theoretical innovations related to the Marshallian theory of the industrial district (i.e. the key role of the nexus local community–industrial development, the scarce relevance of the size of the single firm, the accent upon the alertness – or if we prefer, with Keynes, the "animal spirits" – of the entrepreneurs, and upon the intelligence and honesty of local public servants, etc.), shifting the accent from the mere process of the accumulation of capital to the evolution of all the socio-cultural relationships of the places, opened the way to the modern, interdisciplinary, theory of local development.

---

[29] Cfr. (Whitaker, 1975, vol. 3, pp. 227–228).

7

Trends and Directions in Entrepreneurship Research*

H. E. Aldrich

I have been studying the life and death of small firms for about four decades and I am still fascinated by them. When FSF asked me to speculate about possible new directions for entrepreneurship research, my thoughts first turned to how my own work has changed over the years and where I plan to go next. As one of two sociologists who've won the FSF award, I decided that I should frame my remarks in terms of the contributions of my fellow sociologists, as well as my own work. I believe sociologists have made major contributions toward understanding the conditions under which new organizations are created. Beginning with Weber's analysis of ascetic Protestantism's contributions to the entrepreneurial spirit, sociologists have offered cultural and societal level interpretations of entrepreneurial phenomena. Over the past

* Prepared for FSF 10th Anniversary Celebration, September 19–21, Stockholm.

several decades, with the emergence of entrepreneurship as an academic field, sociological analyses of entrepreneurship have become multifaceted. Today, sociologists conduct multi-level investigations, ranging from the personal networks of individual entrepreneurs to an entire society's transition from socialism to capitalism.

Sociological concern for entrepreneurship can be linked with two themes in recent theory and research. First, entrepreneurs can both reproduce and challenge the existing social order. Stinchcombe (1965) argued that people construct organizations that are culturally embedded and historically specific, reflecting societal conditions at a particular historical conjuncture. Thus, in societies characterized by tendencies toward social inequality in the distribution of income, wealth, political power, and other valued resources, we might expect to see such inequality reproduced within the founding process of new economic organizations. In addition to the potentially reproductive effects of entrepreneur's efforts, linking entrepreneurship to inequality in previous generations, entrepreneurs also affect levels of stratification and inequality in a society by shaping the life chances of founders and their employees. New firms can offer employees jobs tailored to their idiosyncratic skills, rather than requiring them to fit into the pre-existing role structures that characterize large established firms.

Second, entrepreneurship ensures the reproduction of existing organizational populations and lays the foundation for the creation of new populations. Organizational ecologists have mainly focused on dynamics within existing populations, noting that most founding attempts reproduce existing organizational forms and comprise incremental rather than novel additions to the organizational landscape. By contrast, evolutionary theorists have focused on the generation of new populations, analyzing the conditions under which new forms of organizations carve out niches for themselves. Whether a new business simply copies an existing form or strikes off into novel territory depends on the extent to which its founding members possesses diverse outlooks and skills, as well as on the socio-political context in which it is created. Creating entirely new populations requires founding teams that assemble resources in novel ways. Founding teams must also be able to act strategically with other firms to overcome challenges from rival populations and legitimate their own.

These two themes – the relationship between entrepreneurship and the social order, and the role of entrepreneurs in generating novelty at many levels – frame the context within I want to briefly mention three areas where wonderful opportunities exist and where plan to concentrate my own research. Obviously, I hope that other researchers will see the world in similar ways and join me! The three areas are:

(1) the study of entrepreneurial teams;
(2) research on the process by which new firms emerge as coherent entities;
(3) an examination of the link between social inequality and entrepreneurship.

I believe the PSED, championed and nurtured by Paul Reynolds since the mid-1990s, is the single most important data set on entrepreneurship available to researchers today. It will soon be supplemented with PSED2, a project using a similar design but with more cases and questions designed to improve upon those used in the first study. Thus, in my remarks, I will emphasize the role played by the PSED in pushing forward the frontiers of our knowledge concerning entrepreneurship.

7.1 Entrepreneurial Teams

Early writing on entrepreneurial founding teams was either heavily prescriptive – telling founders what they ought to do – or based on analyses of high technology and highly capitalized firms. Those writings emphasized team construction as a pragmatic, instrumental process, with team members recruited on the basis of skills and competencies. Little mention was made of the social embeddedness of entrepreneurial teams. Now, based on research from the PSED on startup team formation, it appears that homophily – the attraction between individuals with shared characteristics – drives the process of matching and forming these teams (Kim and Aldrich, 2005, Ruef *et al.* 2003). In particular, teams are quite homogenous with regard to sex, race, and previous occupation. Our research calls into question the claim that entrepreneurial teams comprise collections of members with diverse and complementary skills.

My colleagues and I have also observed that teams are quite stable over time, and that when they do change, it is in the direction of greater homophily. The strong tendency toward homophily in teams suggests that fundamental social forces within naturally occurring groups may be over-riding founders' instrumental consideration of their teams' compositions. A promising line of investigation concerns the impact of homophily and stability on the tempo of the founding process. If teams form on the basis of homophily, rather than diversity, then what consequences does lack of diversity have for a new venture's survival and growth?

Surprisingly, we have almost no systematic information on the dynamics of team formation and change in startups. In contrast to the planned turnover common in large corporations' top management teams, turnover in new ventures can have immediate and potentially catastrophic consequences. In their early days, new ventures face liabilities of newness that turnover might exacerbate. Moreover, founding team members typically have few employees supporting their actions and thus must rely on their own abilities in the short-term. Thus, the early startup period provides an ideal context for studying the contribution that founders make toward firm performance.

With my colleagues Phillip Kim and Martin Ruef, I am studying how team stability affects the speed at which a founding team achieves various operating milestones. A key milestone during the initial startup phase is the development and institutionalization of core organizational competencies. Following one line of thought, stable teams give nascent firms an advantage because they support efficient and effective coordination among members. Strong working relationships can lead to established core routines if team members remain and a nascent firm builds the necessary combination of relevant skills and experiences. Assuming that the stable team contains members with sufficient internal skills to build a new organization, any turnover represents a loss of momentum. Another line of thought, however, argues that teams repeatedly encounter unforeseen circumstances that might require skills and competencies not possessed by current members. From this viewpoint, turnover enables teams to learn from their experiences, and stable teams thus might signify a team's inability to make strategic changes in its membership. Nascent entrepreneurial team that recruit new or drop existing team members may thus enhance their organizing chances. We hope to discover the conditions under which these scenarios are most likely in a typical startup.

7.2   Emergence: Startups and Human Resources

Human resources are critical for new organizations in ways often unappreciated by theorists who study only established organizations. Founders have trouble establishing a fixed division of labor in young organizations because they are still learning the routines and competencies they need. They must work with the members made available to them by the environment, regardless of their pre-set plans. Moreover, in new and small organizations, rigid job descriptions are a liability when overload and crises occur. Consequently, a new organization's division of labor emerges through a series of local adaptations only partially controlled by founders' plans.

Idiosyncratic jobs thus become embedded early on in an organization's structure, with potentially long-lasting effects. Such jobs generate several significant consequences. First, they increase the level of internal diversity in organizations, which may be an adaptive advantage in changing environments. Second, to the extent they are institutionalized, they allow organizations to retain emergent organizational knowledge that would otherwise be lost. Third, they allow organizations to tap the hidden skills of members. Paradoxically, although developing formerly concealed talents may benefit an organization, it also increases a member's value to other organizations in the population and thus raises turnover rates. Carol Xu and I (2005) are beginning a study on entrepreneurs' potential dependence on key employees that follows up work I began with Ted Baker almost a decade ago (Baker and Aldrich, 1994, 2001).

Given the importance of idiosyncratic jobs, I hope methods should be developed to discover and document them over the next decade. Years later, such jobs will have rationalized myths told about them, as if they were a planned outcome of the founding and growth process. They will thus escape the attention of all but the most persistent researcher who reconstructs an organization's life course. As an antidote, archival and field-based methods have shown some promise. Field methods can capture the jobs as they emerge, but at substantial cost in time and effort. Archival methods are cheaper, but they only imperfectly reflect the existence of idiosyncratic jobs unless founders have been particularly diligent in recording their activities. Process methodologies integrate multiple events at different stages in the startup phase to provide a rich, complex, and realistic understanding of organizational emergence. Carol Xu and I are using a multi-method approach to build a dynamic model of founders' and employees' interactions around a firm's division of labor and its job requirements, and then to test it via simulation, using realistic parameter settings derived from field work and case studies.

7.3   Entrepreneurship and Inequality

In spite of numerous risks, the appeal of being self-employed lures many workers into attempts at starting a new business. This appeal is particularly strong n the United States, where Phillip Kim and I have been studying this process. Buoyed by prospects of greater job autonomy and a chance to be their own boss, workers' drive for social promotion fits into the American ideal of grasping opportunities for advancement and upward social mobility without regard to one's current status. Surveys have repeatedly found that a very high proportion of American workers say that they would like to be self-employed someday. Some immigrant groups view entrepreneurship as a vehicle for integration into the host society, whereas others see business ownership as enabling them to maintain the privileged statuses they occupied in their originating societies.

Aspirations for an entrepreneurial career cut across the occupational spectrum, reflecting the tradition of "ideological equalitarianism" in the United States – a belief in equal access to widely available opportunities (Lipset and Bendix, 1959). However, despite many Americans' expressed desires for being their own boss, only about 10 percent of the

U.S. labor force is self-employed full time. Clearly, many people will be thwarted in their pursuit of an entrepreneurial career. Moreover, nearly four decades of social mobility research have shown that rates of recruitment into self-employment depend heavily on the occupations of one's parents. Some scholars have thus asked whether opportunities to become an entrepreneur are distributed evenly across workers or whether such chances fall disproportionately to those who are already advantaged.

In our research, we are exploring whether wealthy and high-income individuals are more likely to attempt transitions into entrepreneurship than less advantaged individuals. We know that factors other than wealth and income are important in business formation, and thus we have built a general model of nascent entrepreneurship. To the classic sociological concern for wealth and income, we have added two other factors: human and cultural capital. First, with regard to financial capital, if prior wealth or high current income is necessary for starting a business, people who are already advantaged will be most likely to attempt entrepreneurship. Second, having sufficient human capital to begin the organizing process may embolden potential entrepreneurs. Third, individuals contemplating entrepreneurship might benefit from high levels of cultural capital. Obtaining key business skills, especially tacit knowledge, occurs most easily through direct exposure to an entrepreneurial environment, and thus individuals with family business backgrounds will have an advantage over others.

As in many of my other projects, I am using the Panel Study of Entrepreneurial Dynamics in this research project. To fully see the impact of the three forms of capital on people's desires to pursue their entrepreneurial dreams, we need to study people at the earliest stage of the process, when they are still trying to pull their ideas and resources together. Researchers have typically studied entrepreneurs fairly far along in the business formation process, despite the fact that questions about access to entrepreneurship really address behaviors and processes that occur very early in the process. Designs that fail to capture individuals in the early stages of planning their ventures have thus hampered investigators. Some researchers have used cross-section studies to compare self-employed persons with wage and salary workers, whereas others have used longitudinal designs and observed wage and salary workers making successful transitions into self-employment. Studying those who have succeeded, however, does not reveal the characteristics of those who were initially attracted to the role but subsequently failed.

Entrepreneurship in capitalist economies plays a key role in potentially increasing the level of economic inequality – exacerbating stratifying tendencies – because business success is primarily a winner-take-all game. Economic rewards to entrepreneurs stem from their relative performance, compared to other entrepreneurs, rather than the markets economists typically study in which reward mostly depends on absolute performance. For example, a worker's pay depends on his or her productivity, not the production relative to others (in most circumstances). In many high-technology industries, rewards tend to be concentrated in favor of a handful of top performers, further accentuating inequality (Frank and Cook, 1995).

From a policy point of view, "entrepreneurship" itself is amoral, saying nothing about the ends to which entrepreneurs put their resources, once accumulated. If successful entrepreneurs do not recognize the connection between their good fortune and the social structure that made their great rewards possible, they may perceive their gains as entirely their own doing. People who attribute their success only to their own hard work may not be amenable to sharing much of it with their fellow citizens. Thus, a challenge for entrepreneurship researchers in the future may be to figure out how to make entrepreneurs more "humble." That is, to make entrepreneurs more cognizant of the debt they owe to institutional structure and luck, and thus aware also of the interdependence of their fate with that of others.

8

What Have We Learned?

D. Birch

One of the more interesting aspects of the FSF–NUTEK Award is the regular convening of the award winners – usually twice a year. This has been going on for 10 years now; at our last meeting (in the Fall of 2004) it seemed to me that we pulled together a great deal of the collective learning that has occurred. My purposes in this brief paper are: (1) to summarize what I think we are agreed upon, (2) to think a bit about its implications for what countries might do about it, and (3) to reflect on what research priorities for the future might be.

8.1 What We Know

We say it in many ways, but our most important conclusion, in my mind, is that all of our economies are going through a profound transformation of the kind that occurs every 150 or 200 years. Karl-Henrik Pettersson described it as the decline of, first factories, and then Big Old Companies during the 1960s and 1970s, and the emergence of a whole new set of very entrepreneurial firms to replace them. Much of the same thing occurred during the *Industrial Revolution* in the early 1800s, which created the factories and the Big Old Companies. History suggests that the current revolution (which Taichi Sakaiya of Japan aptly calls the *Knowledge-Value Revolution*) will extend for many decades into the future, and that nations that choose to ignore it will suffer badly.

What have we learned about this Revolution?

(1) It is dominated by great turbulence. Company formation and closing rates are increasing rapidly. Product life cycles are getting shorter and shorter (Intel must now replace its entire product line every 18 months).

(2) The phenomenon is occurring in all sectors. Contrary to some public perception, we have had several reports which put the percent of innovative companies that produce new technology ("high-tech" companies) in the 1–3 percent range. The other 97–99 perecnt of innovative companies are appliers of new technologies in virtually every sector of the economy – carpenters, fish wholesalers, shoe manufacturers, dentists, retailers, etc.

(3) Picking winners in this chaotic world is virtually impossible. We have listened to account after account in which private or public attempts to select and fortify winners have failed. The only winning strategy is to let 1000 flowers bloom.

(4) Smaller is dominant. Most successful companies start small, and many stay small. Said another way, the maximum size an average successful company reaches before fading away is getting smaller, the time between startup and fading is getting shorter, and the average annual turnover rate in lists of the largest companies (like the Fortune 500 in the United States) is accelerating rapidly. It used to take 15–20 years for a third of the Fortune 500 to be replaced on the list; it now takes only 3 years.

(5) Much of the inability of larger and successful companies to sustain their success can be traced to rigidity in behavior. Howard Aldrich has reminded us on several occasions that habits are very strong and change very slowly. In a rapidly changing economic environment, slow-to-change habits prove fatal.

(6) Different places are responding very differently to this transformation. This is equally true across countries, and across regions within countries. Paul Reynolds has dramatically documented great variation between countries. Others, including ourselves, the Canadians, the Swedes, and those from Great Britain observe great variation across regions within countries.

(8) Responses to this transformational challenge are deeply cultural. Each of us is just beginning to realize, I think, that different societies view, and value, entrepreneurship in very different ways, and that no one view is better or correct. We are coming to understand that transformation means, almost by definition, instability. Instability, in turn, forces a society to think hard about the value it places on equality (versus inequality), an aggressive (versus courteous) behavior, on the social status of different occupations (doctor, lawyer, government worker, banker, merchant, etc.), and on the role of women in the workplace (to name a few). These value choices a society makes have an enormous bearing on how it will respond to the transformation. Each society must, therefore, work out its own version of a response, and it would be a serious mistake for any society to try to adopt another society's model for its own.

8.2 What Should We Do?

One way or another, we are constantly addressing the question: What should we do? "We" is sometimes a country, sometimes a group of countries (e.g. the European Union), and sometimes a region within a country.

The first and most obvious implication of what we have learned is not to simply adopt some other country's or region's approach. Each country must have its own version, which fits the culture and values of that country. There seem to be a few generalizations that emerge, however:

(1) Increase turbulence, up to, and including, increase failure rates of firms. It seems to be a mistake to try to preserve companies that are not adapting well. We are better off letting them die, and reallocating the people and capital to other, more successful ventures.

(2) Don't try to guess who will succeed. Venture capitalists do this only marginally well, and governments have a pathetic track record when doing it. Let the marketplace decide who will succeed.

(3) Create a supportive environment. There is much that governments can do to improve education (at the elementary, secondary, and university levels), improve air transportation (the Knowledge-Value Economy travels by air), make the tax codes less punitive to risk takers, etc.

(4) Work on the culture. This is a delicate issue, because we believe that each nation has its own culture, and that each must have its own version of Knowledge Value. On the other hand, there are certain basics that must be addressed. Sooner or later entrepreneurs must emerge to bring about the necessary changes. There is much a society can do to recognize and encourage the best and the brightest young people to follow this path, without necessarily dictating how they behave doing it. Recognition alone is worth quite a bit. I received an email from a Swedish journalist in December informing me that Crown Princess Victoria presented the 2004 Gazelle of the Year award to a successful entrepreneur in Sweden. That sends a strong signal to much of Sweden.

(5) Be ready with a plan. Many times a country is doing reasonably well, and is not particularly responsive to a call for change and innovation – particularly when it means changing

the culture in some discernable way. But the time will come when things get worse, when the levels of pain are higher, and when people are looking for answers. Spend your time during good times preparing a plan to be offered in the bad times that will surely follow.

8.3 What to Study

All of the award winners study things; superficially it looks as though each of us studies quite different things. From my perspective, however, we are each looking at the same thing from different angles. That said, we do have different kinds of expertise, and we need to reflect a bit on which angles are needed the most.

My angle is to count. It is to try to document the role that entrepreneurs play in economies, particularly as they relate to growth and job creation. I think we continue to need some of that in order to have some bases for informing the rest of society about the important roe that small and growing companies play in most countries. If they are not important, then everything else is pretty much a waste of time.

Counting them up, however, tells you very little about what makes them tick. Understanding what makes them tick would be my top research priority for the future. Most of the discussion I hear about how to encourage entrepreneurs and entrepreneurship reflects very little understanding about what goes on inside the head of an entrepreneur. What kind of a person is likely to be good at it? How are those who wish to grow a company different from those who wish merely to have one? How can we use this knowledge to help people judge for themselves whether or not they ought to try it? How can we use this knowledge to guide our education system to be more relevant? For example, in my view (with my entrepreneur hat on) the least useful, and most often taught, business skill is accounting. Any successful entrepreneur can quickly hire someone to keep score (i.e. do accounting). Yet many educational systems use accounting as a litmus test to decide whether a student will get more business education – much as biochemistry is used as a filter for future potential doctors. We ought to be able to do better than that – much better.

8.4   In Sum

It's been a very interesting 10 years. What's been remarkable about them, from my perspective, is how differently the participants viewed the world entering the process, and how much we seem to have converged on the common understandings which I have attempted to summarize herein. Said another way, we each seem to have learned a lot. I am sure that not everyone will agree with everything I have said. But I think most would agree with most of what I have said, and, given where we all started – coming from very different cultures and skill sets – that is quite remarkable, and worthy of note.

9

Understanding Entrepreneurship: Achievements and Opportunities – A Personal Assessment*

P. D. Reynolds

Developing specialization in economic activities – and reciprocal trading of complementary goods and services – has been a major human pastime ever since there were humans. Perhaps these became "businesses" when the trades occurred outside the immediate family or kinship group, when a farmer traded grain for a hunter's recent kill. The differentiation, specialization, reciprocal trading, and interdependence – usually mediated by a monetary system – are major economic activities in all countries; the most complex systems and networks are found in the most developed societies.

The study of large organizations – government agencies or private businesses – has been a central focus of scholarly research and policy

---

* A commentary prepared for the 10th Annual SFS–NUTEK International Award for Entrepreneurship and Small Business Research.

development for centuries. While their have been a number of scholarly commentaries on new firm creation and entrepreneurship – Weber and Schumpeter come immediately to mind – serious empirical work on the role and contribution of new and small firms seems to have started in the late 1960s. The initial assessments of sources of job growth in the U.S. economy by David Birth were critical in directing attention to the role and contributions of new and growing firms. But the empirical work has seriously outrun the capacity to develop a formalized conceptual scheme – or theory – that can encompass the dynamic nature of economies with the constant churning of firms and jobs, much less the shifts in the productive and organizational systems as they adapt to new technologies and demands for different goods and services.

For those committed to the creation of empirically based knowledge, the ultimate goal is a relatively close correspondence between the body of empirical work and conceptual frameworks or formal theories that may develop among scholars. In terms of the study of new and small firms, the substantial expansion of empirical research over the past several decades has far outstripped the conceptual schemes available to provide a complete understanding or explaining of the phenomena.

A number of patterns – empirical generalizations or stylized facts – continue to appear in research. These are presented in three categories based on the unit of analysis: (1) a social or economic aggregate – geographically bounded system (region, nation, etc.) or an economic sector; (2) the firm or a "firm-in-creation" by an individuals or team of individuals, and (3) human actors participating in firm creation or management.

(A) *System patterns*

- New firms are a major source of new jobs; the other major sources are new branches and subsidiaries of existing firms.
- High rates of new firm formation have a strong association with aggregate economic growth: country, region, market sector, etc.
- New firms are a major source of increased productivity in most sectors.

- New firms have a major role in the process of economic adaptation and change.
- Strong correlations exist between firm births and firm deaths.
- Higher rates of churning and turbulence and growth are associated with higher levels of subsequent economic growth.
- Regional, contextual characteristics have a major impact on the level of business creation of a geographic area or economic sector.
- In most advanced economies, the total number of firms continues to increase, the average size of firms and establishments decreases, and firms and establishments are becoming more specialized. The level of interdependence among businesses continues to increase.

(B) *Business activity as the unit of analysis*

- The immediate regional context has a major impact on the emergence of new firms.
- About one in three nascent firms (in the startup phase) become operating new businesses.
- Median time to complete the startup process with a new firm is 12–18 months; the range is 1 to 300 months.
- A small proportion of new firms, less than 1 in 5, will have high growth; growth trajectories vary substantially, for many firms' periods of rapid growth are separated by periods of stability.
- Less than 1 in 20 new firms expect to have a major impact on the structure of economic markets – the goods and services provided.
- Less than 1 in 20 new firms – in production, distribution, or final delivery – are based on major advances in new technology.
- Firms changing the market structure and implementing new technology are usually not the same firms.
- From 30 to 50 percent of new firms are implemented by a family or kinship unit and, as a result, are usually emphasizing

two – often incompatible – objectives, maximizing economic and family values. This is not always achieved.

- Major source of financing are informal funds provided by family, friends, colleagues; the aggregate amount is equivalent to that provided by traditional financial institutions and 5–30 times that provided by venture capitalists.
- New firms are added to official registries at different points in the startup process; in no two countries are the procedures comparable.
- All firms die, the major issues are when and under what conditions.

(C) *Individual behavior as a unit of analysis*

- People create new firms, alone or in teams.
- Participating in new firm creation is a major career option pursued by adults in the workforce all over the world.
- The global level of firm startup participation is enormous, approximately half a billion adults, 1 in 12 of the world population.
- Active participation in new firm creation varies dramatically among countries, from less than 1 in 20 to more than 1 in 3 adults in the workforce age period.
- About one-third of the world population of nascent entrepreneurs is involved through lack of employment opportunities – necessity entrepreneurs; the remainder – opportunity entrepreneurs – are seeking to take advantage of a business opportunity.
- Men are about twice as likely to be involved as women in new firm creation; most of the activity is pursued by young and mid-life adults.
- Necessity entrepreneurs generally have less education and less access to resources than opportunity entrepreneurs; but motivation may adjust if the firm is successful.
- People working on and for new firms have higher moral than those working with or for large formalized organizations.

Given this emerging pattern of "facts" about the entrepreneurial process and new firm creation, what are the most promising avenues for future scholarship and data collection? Four types of activities – related to scholarly or practical concerns – can be considered: (i) conceptual or theoretical development; (ii) contributions to data collection and measurement; (iii) improvements in defining the relevant populations and obtaining representative samples; and (iv) significant research programs.

9.1 Conceptual Development

Conceptual or theoretical work should make a distinction between economic systems at different levels of development. Clearly the role of the entrepreneurial sector in an advanced economy is a distinctive challenge. A conceptualization that can encompass both a static overview of a complex economic system as well as the contributions of a turbulent entrepreneurial sector, where a major of participants are pursuing new business opportunities, that leads changes in market structures and productivity improvements would be a major contributions to understanding. More precise abstract conceptualizations of high technology, high market impact, and high growth would be an important part of such a conceptual scheme. Such conceptualizations might consider the relative benefits in having the future structure and form of the economic system determined through the entrepreneurial process, compared to formal national government decisions that are then imposed on the entrepreneurial sector.

However, it may require a somewhat different conceptual scheme for considering the role of entrepreneurship in developing countries. These would be countries with a level of resources and productivity to facilitate basic investments in health, education, and legal and physical infrastructures. Marginal economic systems, where day-to-day survival is uncertain, are a different matter; a daily scramble for food does not allow for much of the future planning or resource hoarding required for firm creation. In developing countries, up to half of the startup efforts reflect the lack of other work options and a substantial proportion of new business ideas may be imported from developed countries.

Nonetheless, the presence of a vigorous entrepreneurial sector seems to be associated with economic advancement. A more precise conceptualization of this process – including the contributions of both opportunity and necessity entrepreneurship – would be a considerable contribution.

9.2   Measurement and Indicators

There are a number of concepts for which both abstract definitions and operational procedures are widely accepted, such as gross domestic product (GDP), unemployment, and the family. A number of concepts widely used in the study of entrepreneurial phenomenon have yet to reach a high level of consensus; perhaps most central is the amorphous, multifaceted "image" of entrepreneurship. As a result, when there are efforts to conduct research, there is no well-accepted measure of entrepreneurship or firm creation, based on either a single indicator or a set of related indicators. The same problems confront efforts to track firm development over the business life course. The basic stages – initiation (or conception), startup (or gestation), birth (or transition) to an operating entity, as well as growth (measured by jobs, assets, profits, or market share) and "disengagement" (termination or firm death) – remain appealing as general concepts, but have no universally accepted empirical indicators. If entrepreneurship is to be applied only to those efforts that are innovative or related to high growth aspirations, then clear operational procedures for identifying the presence of both – innovativeness, growth – would also be of great value.

Similar problems are associated with a range of other features, such as the startup (or founding) team, high technology, and market impact. Equally significant are defining the boundaries of a firm, which is traditionally done in terms of a physical location, although those with multiple locations – or that small proportion with no fixed location – become a challenge. There is also the familiar "establishment–enterprise" distinction. How to determine when a set of establishments – each a separate physical productive unit – should be considered a single enterprise, participating in a common strategy and sharing resources? A similar complication is present in determining the organizational boundaries of special types of organizations – such as franchises and multilevel marketing networks – where each unit may be treated as a separate legal entity but their entire set engaged in coordinated, focused behavior and may share (or pool) resources to achieve objectives. Lack of agreement on identifying the boundaries of existing business organizations makes it difficult to distinguish new firms from expansion of an existing multiunit firm.

9.3 Defining Relevant Populations

There are a number of different units of analysis relevant to entrepreneurial phenomena: people, business entities, markets (economic sectors), and geographic regions.

As units of analysis, the human population is the easiest to define; there is, however, the issue of who is to be considered a central participant in the entrepreneurial process. Restricting focus to those actively involved in firm creation with expectations of some ownership role has been well received. Some have expanded this to include those accepting responsibility for major startup functions, without expectations of ownership and others have expanded this even further to include helpful persons in the social networks of the core entrepreneurial team.

There is more diversity regarding the actual business entity – how it is to be identified, related to definitional problems reviewed above. Clarity regarding that point in the startup process when a "discussion topic" because a "business initiative" with a life of its own – independent of any one person – has yet to be resolved. A different dimension is represented by assessments based on the variation in ownership by private individuals (startup team and financial sponsors) versus existing business organizations, which can vary from complete support from private sources to complete support from existing businesses with many receiving a mixture of both.

There are many reasons to focus on the impact of entrepreneurial processes on a given economic sector or market – exchanges focusing on a well-defined category of goods or services. In some cases the markets are very local – such as housing in a single geographic area – and in other cases they may be global in nature – such as a specialized software application that can be delivered over the worldwide Internet. Different definitions of markets will lead to different assessments of entrepreneurship.

The geographic context of entrepreneurial processes may be a single sub-national region, an entire nation, or a region of the world. Each type of region may be defined in different ways, but cultural history and political acceptability is the usual basis for such definitions. Nations, in particular, are a source of considerable contextual factors that can affect the appearance and impact of entrepreneurial processes; exploring diversity of context within countries requires a procedure for defining sub-national regions. This issue is particularly complicated when a supra-national structure becomes involved in efforts to standardize sub-national classifications among a set of countries, as with EU countries.

9.4   Research Programs

There are a number of important empirical patterns related to entrepreneurship and new firm creation; many are associated in interesting and statistically significant ways. Determining causal relationships is of considerable importance. The strongest confidence in causal relationships is based on experimental designs, where researchers deliberately vary the context or impact on different entities and observe the subsequent differences among the entities. Such a research design is unlikely to be possible for most entrepreneurial phenomena; the resources required would be enormous, the practical problems of administration would be considerable, and in most cases the design would not meet current standards for ethical research.

This leaves two traditional research designs for exploring entrepreneurship; one is cross-section comparisons at the same point in time and the other are longitudinal assessments of the same units at different points in time. All researches are based on comparisons and unless there is some variation the comparisons are of little value. In both of these designs variation in both independent and dependent variables are provided by natural processes in the relevant human, organizational, and social (economic systems). The researcher is primarily involved in data collection – measuring things and events as they develop. Causality is inferred from examination of temporal sequences and attempts to estimate the impact of alternative mechanisms on the dependent variable.

In terms of entrepreneurial phenomena, two major issues seem to justify substantial research investments. One is an examination of contextual factors – national, sub-national regions, sectorial – on the emergence and nature of entrepreneurial activities and, in turn, the impact of entrepreneurial activities on the context, presumably in a later period. Such efforts require harmonized measures of all critical variables across the units in the study – national, regions, sectors; this implies a great deal of operational coordination to standardize both the measures of interest as well as those factors that would represent other processes that may affect the major independent variable – entrepreneurship or economic growth. There are, fortunately, a number of international programs that assemble standardized data on basic national characteristics, although formal listings of both firms and new firm creation have not yet achieved an acceptable level of harmonization across national data sets. Though expensive and complicated to implement, it is now technically feasible to implement cross-national surveys of the presence of entrepreneurial activities, providing approximate estimates to very important issues. In such efforts the region, nation, or sector is the unit of analysis and the assessments are based on repeated measures captured at different points in time.

Tracking the details of the entrepreneurial process – as individuals on their own or sponsored by existing businesses – move thorough the early stages of the firm life course involves a somewhat different type of effort. In this case a procedure must be developed to identify the individuals (alone or in teams) as they enter the startup phase and proceed to organize and implement a new business. Such efforts, if to be based on representative samples, can be somewhat expensive but yield invaluable information regarding who creates new firms and how they proceed. Substantial experience with such research protocols has accumulated in the last decade – projects have been implemented in over half a dozen countries – and it is clear that such efforts are feasible, affordable, and provide a wealth of useful information relevant to both scholarly understanding and practical issues. There does not yet appear to be a set of coordinated, harmonized national projects tracking the details of the entrepreneurial process. It is of some interest to determine if the entrepreneurial process takes different forms in different countries.

In conclusion, it would seem that substantial progress has been made in the exploration of the entrepreneurial process in the past several decades. Not only have a number of empirical regularities been established, there has been progress in developing operational definitions that provide widely accepted measures of entrepreneurial activity. Several very useful research designs have received considerable field testing and demonstrated their financial and operational viability. A number of empirical patterns continue to recur in these projects. Entrepreneurship research has gone well beyond the explanatory capacity of existing theoretical structures; there is much room for improvement in the relevant theories.

10

A "Critical Mess" Approach to Entrepreneurship Scholarship

W. B. Gartner

It is a capital mistake to theorize before one has data. Insensibly one begins to twist the facts to suit theories, instead of theories to suit facts.

Arthur Conan Doyle

My perspective on future trends in the field of entrepreneurship focuses on an idea, that, at the current moment, seems to be intriguing, to me, and, I hope, of interest to others. My fascination with entrepreneurship is in entrepreneurship, itself. By "entrepreneurship, itself," I mean I am curious about the study of all things that seem to be about entrepreneurship, as a phenomenon. But I am not, necessarily, curious about studying entrepreneurship solely from a phenomenological perspective. The idea that is presented, here, explores the approach that I take to the study of entrepreneurship, which is labeled the "critical mess." The idea of the "critical mess" is less of a coherent methodology for studying entrepreneurship, and more of a nuance toward the kinds of facts and theories that one might use for understanding what "entrepreneurship, itself," actually is, or might be.

I may be, at this moment in the history of the FSF–NUTEK Awards, unique among the award winners in that my research on entrepreneurship does not seem to be easily categorized into a particular disciplinary perspective, such as economics, sociology, or psychology. By starting with the question, "What is entrepreneurship?" the answers to exploring this question begin with descriptions of the phenomenon. From description, one might then begin to offer ideas as to "why" aspects of the phenomenon behave as they do. (This approach, I believe, is somewhat similar to naturalistic inquiry (Lincoln and Guba, 1985), but, as I hope to show, also different, in that I'm less concerned with the facts generated from direct personal experience.) As the quote that begins this article suggests, the primacy of facts should drive the search for theory that can make sense of those facts. The trend that is currently occurring in entrepreneurship scholarship is for many scholars to import a theory from another discipline and then go in search of facts to support it. When scholars are grounded in the facts of their own discipline and the facts found in the entrepreneurship area, then, the application of theories from other disciplines results in the kinds of insightful ideas that other FSF–NUTEK award winners have found. But, when scholars are not well grounded in the facts of a particular discipline (e.g., "non-disciplined trained" entrepreneurship scholars who inappropriately apply a theory from a discipline outside of entrepreneurship), or when scholars are not well grounded in the facts of entrepreneurship (e.g., "disciplined trained" scholars who inappropriately apply entrepreneurship facts to their theories), we get confusion, rather than insight. My approach is to ask scholars to devote substantially more time to collecting and being "mindful" (Langer, 1979) of facts about entrepreneurship, before identifying a theory to find causal linkages among these facts. The remainder of this article will describe the "critical mess" approach, and then, offer other analogies as attempts to capture the sensibility in the perspective I propose.

10.1   The "Critical Mess" Approach

I came across the label "critical mess" in reading an article on book collecting in *The New Yorker* magazine that Sue Birley and I subsequently used as an analogy for the value of qualitative research in the field of entrepreneurship (Gartner and Birley, 2002, p. 394).

> Finally, we offer an insight about the nature of qualitative research which might be considered as a parting trifle, but we believe contains some truth which bears consideration: the "critical mess theory." In qualitative research there is typically an immersion into the muddled circumstances of an entrepreneurial phenomenon that is cluttered and confusing. Part of the difficulty of generating and reporting the findings of a qualitative research effort seems to stem from the experience of being in such an untidy reality. Qualitative researchers seem to get overwhelmed with too much information, rather than too little. Yet, it is in this experience of information overload that a certain knowledge and wisdom often occurs. One can often tell which researchers in our field have spent considerable time intensively involved with entrepreneurs. The knowledge and insights that stem from all of their research just seem to ring a bit truer and clearer. We borrow a label for this sensibility of immersion from a profile of Michael Zinman, a bibliophile and Michael Reese's insights into Zinman's strategy for collecting books:
>
>> "You don't start off with a theory about what you're trying to do. You don't begin by saying, 'I'm trying to prove x.' You build a big pile. Once you get a big enough pile together – the critical mess – you're able to draw conclusions about it. You see patterns... People who have the greatest intuitive feel for physical objects start from a relationship with

the objects and then acquire the scholarship, instead of the other way around. The way to become a connoisseur is to work in the entire spectrum of what's available – from utter crap to fabulous stuff. If you're going to spend your time looking only at the best, you're not going to have a critical eye." (Singer, 2001, p. 66).

Qualitative researchers are likely to be the connoisseurs of entrepreneurship scholarship only in that they are more likely to immerse themselves to a greater depth and in a wider variety of situations where entrepreneurship occurs. We encourage all entrepreneurship scholars to develop a critical eye in their efforts to explore entrepreneurship, and hope that more work will be undertaken to utilize qualitative methods for seeking such an understanding.

The "critical mess" label has captured my imagination for providing a way for me to talk about the diverse ways I have looked at entrepreneurship, itself (Gartner, 2004). My original research sought to create a "critical mess" of information (based on data from 106 questionnaires and "mini-cases" written from in-depth interviews) that resulted in a typology of ways that individuals start businesses (Gartner *et al.*, 1989), and I have used similar quantitative/qualitative "messes" to look at individuals starting businesses during the evolution of the fresh-squeezed orange juice industry (Duchesneau and Gartner, 1990), and the stories of entrepreneurs in magazine articles (Gartner *et al.*, 1999). Probably the biggest quantitative/qualitative "critical mess" is the Panel Study of Entrepreneurial Dynamics (PSED), which is a longitudinal generalizable sample of individuals in the process of starting businesses (Gartner *et al.*, 2004). I have also been interested in how the imagination, through fiction, provides insights into entrepreneurship: for example, the *Music Man* as "corporate entrepreneur" (Gartner *et al.*, 1985), *Pilgrim's Progress* as an entrepreneurial odyssey (Gartner *et al.*, 1987; and studies of the importance of human volition through entrepreneurial action using the films

Ikiru (Gartner, 1990b) and *The Man Who Planted Trees* (Gartner, 1993b). And, I have been interested in how entrepreneurship scholars make sense of entrepreneurship as an academic field (Gartner, 1990a, 2001), and how poetry and art might offer a language for describing the process of organizing (Gartner, 1993a). This eclectic selection of examples is a mess: no one particular theoretical perspective, no one particular kind or type of data, and fiction seems to have as much value for providing insights into entrepreneurship, as empirical facts. There is much to recommend for taking this approach.

I find that scholars who use a rather narrow disciplinary focus in the field of entrepreneurship often lack the "critical eye" that comes from creating a "critical mess." It is all too easy to use the "fabulous stuff" in one's own discipline without attending to the "utter crap" that might be found in other disciplines or in other research findings in one's own discipline, as well. Without a deep and comprehensive understanding and appreciation of the breadth and complexity of entrepreneurship scholarship (as well as other non-scholarly work about entrepreneurship), it is easy to generate results that seem to look right (given the theory and evidence used), yet are wrong to anyone with a broader knowledge of the phenomenon of entrepreneurship, itself.

10.2 Conventional Wisdom versus Esoteric Knowledge

In somewhat the same vein, Davis (1971) in "That's Interesting!" suggests this conflict about acquiring a broad range of facts versus a focus on theory is inherent between laypersons with "conventional wisdom" and experts with "esoteric knowledge":

> "Intellectual specialties were formed when various groups of self-styled experts began to accept those propositions which had refuted the assumptions of laymen. As an intellectual speciality developed, what began merely as a proposition which refuted a taken-for-granted assumption of the common-sense world now became a taken-for-granted assumption in its own right. When an intellectual speciality reached maturity – and

> this is the important point – all propositions generated
> within it are referred back not to the old baseline of
> the take-for-granted assumption of the common-sense
> world, but to the new baseline of the take-for-granted
> assumption of the intellectual speciality itself (Davis,
> 1971, p. 330).

Something gets lost when the focus of research on entrepreneurship
sticks too closely to the "esoteric knowledge" a narrow disciplinary
perspective. A finding can be right and interesting to a scholar within
a specific theoretical perspective, but, wrong or obvious to the practitioner and scholar with a broader and messier knowledge of the phenomenon. If scholarship in the field of entrepreneurship emphasizes the
search for answers using narrow disciplinary approaches, we may find
ourselves irrelevant to the issues facing those persons involved in the
broader phenomenon of entrepreneurship, itself.

10.3 Hedgehogs versus Foxes

Another metaphor that captures aspects of the "critical mess" approach
from the perspective of a cognitive orientation is Isaiah Berlin's expo-
sition on the hedgehog and the fox (Berlin, 1993, p. 1):

> There is a line among the fragments of the Greek
> poet Archilochus which says: 'The fox knows many
> things, but the hedgehog knows one big thing'. Scholars
> have differed about the correct interpretation of these
> dark words, which may mean no more than that the
> fox, for all his cunning, is defeated by the hedgehog's
> one defense. But, taken figuratively, the words can be
> made to yield a sense in which they mark one of the
> deepest differences which divide writers and thinkers,
> and, it may be, human beings in general. For there
> exists a great chasm between those, on one side, who
> relate everything to a single central vision, one system
> less or more coherent or articulate, in terms of which
> they understand, think and feel – a single, universal,

organizing principle in terms of which alone all that they are and say has significance – and, on the other side, those who pursue many ends, often unrelated and even contradictory, connected, if at all, only in some *de facto* way, for some psychological or physiological cause, related by no moral or aesthetic principle; these last lead lives, perform acts, and entertain ideas that are centrifugal rather than centripetal, their thought is scattered or diffused, moving on many levels, seizing upon the essence of a vast variety of experiences and objects for what they are in themselves, without consciously or unconsciously, seeking to fit them into, or exclude them from, any one unchanging, all-embracing, sometimes self-contradictory and incomplete, at times fanatical, unitary inner vision. The first kind of intellectual and artistic personality belongs to the hedgehogs, the second to the foxes ...."

This dichotomy (the fox of "many things" versus the hedgehog of "one big thing") has actually been the subject of much serious academic study in regards to the kinds of cognitive styles individuals use for making judgments and forecasts (*cf.*, Suedfeld and Tetlock, 2002). In general, the "fox" cognitive style appears to lead to better predictions and judgments compared to the "hedgehog" style. Indeed, Tetlock (2005), in a summary of 20 years of research on the judgment of political experts, describes a number of ways that foxes appear to differ from hedgehogs that would seem to bolster the value of the "critical mess" approach.

Foxes are more skeptical about the use of theory to explain the past or predict the future. One of the problems with applying theory is that application requires judgment about which theories would actually be relevant in particular situations. Yet, theorists tend to seek parsimony in their explanations, so that "one size fits all" more often becomes "all sizes fit one." By being more mindful of all of the facts that accumulate in the "critical mess" there is less of a temptation to seize on a singular explanation.

Foxes tend to qualify predictions with disconfirming evidence. A "critical mess" of information is more likely to keep one humble when positing a particular theory to explain these facts. This sensibility is also, I believe, a characteristic of the practitioner's conventional wisdom. The day-to-day bombardment of disparate facts stemming from being in the phenomenon of entrepreneurship does not often lend itself to "a theory" that can encompass one's particular situation.

Foxes are more likely to see the ironic aspects of the phenomenon, in that irony enables one to see the double meanings as well as the paradoxes imbedded in the situation. An example that comes to mind about the irony inherent in entrepreneurship would be the paradox of entrepreneurs as self-seeking individuals. We assume that entrepreneurs are more likely to be self-actualizers, individuals who "do their own thing" yet, those individuals we are likely to suggest as exemplars of entrepreneurship (e.g., Bill Gates and Richard Branson) are wildly successful because they provide goods and services that other people want. So, success in entrepreneurship at "doing your own thing" requires that this doing be about solving other people's problems. Indeed, I believe that entrepreneurship is actually based more in irony than other "personal"-oriented activities, such as the creation of art (*cf.*, Hjorth). Entrepreneurship, inherently involves the "other." Entrepreneurial activity requires transaction and interaction (Katz and Gartner, 1988) among a variety of people, while it is possible to create art without patrons, buyers or an audience. A "critical mess" approach that begins with the phenomenon, itself, is more likely to recognize the many different facets of particular entrepreneurial actions and their many possible meanings. Probably the best proponents of an ironical approach to the study of entrepreneurship are works by Hjorth (2003) and Steyaert (1995, 1997), where their ability to explore the subtle dualities in the phenomenon of entrepreneurship are magical.

Foxes are more likely to see the "and" among competing points of view rather than posit the "either/or." I suggest that one important feature of a "critical mess" approach is a willingness to see entrepreneurship across multiple levels of analysis (Davidsson and Wiklund, 2001). So, for example, it is valuable to be able to see that individual action takes place within a social and environmental context, and, to appreciate how the individual might influence the social/environment and vice versa.

Finally, a quote from Tetlock (2005, p. 118) on some problematic aspects of the hedgehog approach:

> "... hedgehogs dig themselves into intellectual holes. The deeper they dig, the harder it gets to climb out and see what is happening outside, and the more tempting it becomes to keep on doing what they know how to do; continue their metaphorical digging by uncovering new reasons why their initial inclination, usually too optimistic or pessimistic, was right. Hedgehogs are thus at continual risk of becoming prisoners of their preconceptions, trapped in self-reinforcing cycles in which their initial ideological disposition stimulates thoughts that further justify that inclination, which, in turn, stimulates further supportive thoughts."

The challenge, then, is to keep oneself open to a variety of facts and ideas that may become apparent through mindful experience (Langer, 1979). I find that my greatest challenge as an entrepreneurship researcher [as in re- (go back) search- (and look)] is to pay attention to entrepreneurship scholarship across a wider venue of disciplines and perspectives, and to read comprehensively, rather than selectively.

10.4 Complicate Yourself!

The title of my speech at the FSF–NUTEK award ceremony was "Entrepreneurship in Two Words of Less" and the presentation was based on four slogans that I had printed on T-shirts to both show and give away. (I find that there are fewer technical glitches with showing a T-shirt compared to using a computer to display PowerPoint slides.) The four slogans were: [ ] THINK; Aspire Higher; Fail *forward;* and Complicate Yourself! Social psychologists will be familiar with "Complicate Yourself!" as the final section heading in Weick's *Social Psychology of Organizing* (Weick, 1979). My "takeaway" from Weick's

"Complicate Yourself!" slogan is that complex phenomena require complex people:

> "... the complicated individual can sense variations in a larger environment, select what need *not* be attended to, what will *not* change imminently, what *won't* happen, and by this selection the individual is able to amplify his control variety. He safely (that is, insightfully) ignores that which will not change, concentrates on that which will, and much like the neurotic psychiatrist is able to anticipate significant environmental variation when and where it occurs. Complicated observers take in more. They see patterns that less complicated people miss, and they exploit these subtle patterns by concentrating on them and ignoring everything else."
> (Weick, 1979, 193)

The phenomenon of entrepreneurship is complicated (Gartner, 1985), and, for this reason, I believe, the "critical mess" approach is a necessary bromide to narrower disciplinary perspectives. As I suggested at the beginning of this article, those entrepreneurship scholars with an omnivorous willingness to collect facts and ideas: both good and bad; "utter crap to fabulous stuff;" micro and macro; individual, firm and environment; esoteric knowledge and conventional wisdom; the pedantic and amateur; policy and personal, are more likely to develop the discernment so necessary for finding the key nuggets of insight about entrepreneurship as a phenomenon. The challenge, then, for entrepreneurship scholars, is to be willing to build their own "big pile" of knowledge, facts, theories, experiences, and insights about the phenomenon of entrepreneurship, and to be at peace with the realization that much of what one collects is "utter crap." The process of developing insight is not efficient. And, there is no guarantee that there will be fabulous stuff buried within one's mess. But, such efforts are necessary.

11

A Formulation of Entrepreneurship Policy

Z. J. Acs

11.1 Introduction

In industrial society wealth creation, wealth ownership, and wealth distribution were in part left up to the state. However, in an entrepreneurial society it is individual initiative that plays a vital role in propelling the system forward. We cast the United States as the first new nation, the product of a shift in human character and social role that produced the English Revolution and Modern American Civilization. It was the working out of this new character type, *the agent*, who possessed unprecedented new powers of discretion and self-reliance, yet was bound to collective ends by novel emerging forms of institutional authority and internal restraint, that set the stage for an entrepreneurial society.

Entrepreneurial leadership is the mechanism by which new combinations are created, new markets are opened up and new technologies are commercialized that are the basis for prosperity. In an entrepreneurial society, entrepreneurship plays a vital role in the process of wealth creation and philanthropy plays a crucial role in the reconstitution of wealth. In other words, the entrepreneurship–philanthropy nexus is the institutional arrangement that maintains the circular flow of wealth creation and reconstitution, through a positive feedback mechanism that ensures the continued economic, cultural, and social development of an entrepreneurial society.

We define entrepreneurship very broadly as *the process by which agents transform knowledge into wealth through new firm formation and growth, and then reconstitute wealth into opportunity for all through philanthropy.* This formulation involves four broad levels of actors in an entrepreneurial society. First, individual *agents* identify business opportunities and make the personal choice to exploit them. Second, newly formed *businesses* innovate, using knowledge and other resources to produce new services and products. Third, the *economy* includes all those institutions that play an important role in economic development and productivity growth. Finally *society*, as the collection of all agents, and the ultimate beneficiary from the increased wealth, plays a central role in social progress and equity, by reconstituting a share of new wealth through philanthropy to create opportunity for others.

Each one of these facets has an appropriate policy counterpart in an entrepreneurial society. The individual agent is confronted with education and occupational choice policies that govern the boundaries by which individuals can make occupational choices. At the business level governments pursue enabling policies that facilitate or restrict the formation of new firms. At the level of the economy supporting policies foster the growth of businesses, and thereby the growth of the economy. Finally, societies are sustained by social policies that are incorporated into their legal structures and regulations to ensure their continued functioning. This formulation gives rise to a corresponding set of goals that are at the heart of an entrepreneurial society: *more effective entrepreneurship, continuous innovation, faster economic growth, and social equity.* While these policies can be pursued independently at the agency level they cannot be pursued independently at the social level.

11.2 Entrepreneurship and Occupational Choice Policy

The first facet of entrepreneurial policy focuses on the individual agent.

This so-called occupational choice question has been examined by at least three disciplines. First, the sociology literature offers explanations for entrepreneurship, which include ethnic cultural attitudes and lack of alternative employment opportunities due to lack of appropriate education or language skills among some groups of Americans and immigrants.

The psychology literature focuses primarily on cognitive conditions in the individual agent, and has extended this to include demographic conditions in the individual–opportunity nexus. The psychology literature has shown that people who engage in entrepreneurial activity are not randomly determined, but tend to share certain individual-level characteristics.

The economic literature focuses on the occupational choice question. The decision confronting each agent, to become either an employee in an incumbent enterprise or an entrepreneur starting a new firm, depends on the expected risk-adjusted profit accruing from such a new firm compared to the expected wage from employment. Certainly these expected returns would differ according to the educational attainment of the potential entrepreneur and the occupational field. The very low expected wages usually earned by high school dropouts may explain the positive relationship we found between entrepreneurship rates and share of such dropouts.

The occupational choice facet of entrepreneurship policy focuses on individual agents, rather than businesses. Limiting it to this facet, focuses entrepreneurship policy on those measures intended to directly influence the level of entrepreneurial vitality in a country or a region. However, the sociological and psychological aspects of occupational choice are not subject to change except by very long-term policies. The expectations built into the economic analysis of occupational choice are also difficult to change, but many of the recently developed entrepreneurial education programs are showing some successes at teaching the skills and confidence necessary for successful entrepreneurship, assuming possession of some economically valuable idea on which to build an innovative new business.

Some of these courses operate at the elementary or secondary school level, serving primarily to draw attention to entrepreneurship as a potential choice, and perhaps teaching the students to be attentive for knowledge spillovers that might provide the basis for an innovative new business. Others serve either business school students or students of the sciences, cultivating their interest, skills, and confidence for pursuing their own business opportunities.

11.3   Entrepreneurship and Enabling Policies

The second facet of entrepreneurial policy has to do with enabling policies. Such policies are targeted to enhance the spillover of knowledge and focus on enabling the commercialization of knowledge, which frequently results in new-firm formation. Such enabling policies are increasingly at the state, regional, or even local level, outside of the jurisdiction of the traditional federal regulatory and support agencies.

The greatest and most salient shift in small- and medium-sized enterprises (SME) policy over the past 15 years has been the gradual shift of government from trying to preserve and expand SMEs that are confronted with a cost, financing, or market handicap due to size-inherent-scale disadvantages, toward promoting startup and growth of small entrepreneurial firms involved in the commercialization of new knowledge, often new technology-based firms. It is important to point out that entrepreneurship and innovation go together, since almost all new firm startups are innovative to some degree. Therefore most policies for support of research also contribute, directly or indirectly, to the new firm formation rate in the United States.

These programs promoting entrepreneurship in a regional context are typical of the new enabling policies to promote entrepreneurial activity. While these entrepreneurial policies are evolving, they are clearly gaining in importance and impact in the overall portfolio of economic policy instruments. Whether they will ultimately prove to be successful remains the focus of coming research. The point to be emphasized in this paper is that entrepreneurship policies are important instruments in the arsenal of policies to promote growth.

They represent an alternative not only to the set of instruments implied in the neoclassical growth theory, but also to the limitations of endogenous growth theory. As this book suggests, while generating knowledge and human capital may be a necessary condition for economic growth, it is not sufficient. Rather, a supplementary set of policies focusing on enhancing the conduits of knowledge spillovers also plays a central role in promoting economic growth.

11.4 Entrepreneurship and Supporting Policies

The third facet of entrepreneurship policy applies to the whole economy. How can we help new firms to grow? The policy focus of the neoclassical growth models was on deepening capital and augmenting it with labor. Thus, the policy debate revolved around the efficacy of instruments designed to induce capital investment, such as low interest rates and tax credits, along with instruments to reduce the cost of labor, such as reduced income and payroll taxes, and increased labor market mobility.

A significant and compelling contribution of the endogenous growth theory was to refocus the policy debate away from the emphasis on enhancing capital and labor, to a new priority on increasing knowledge and human capital – the main engine of growth is the accumulation of human capital – of knowledge – and the main source of differences in living standards among nations is differences in human capital. Physical capital accumulation plays an essential but decidedly subsidiary role. Thus, the debate on policies to generate growth revolved around the efficacy of such instruments as universities, secondary schools, public and private investments in research and development (R&D), training programs, and apprentice systems.

If new firm formation is a necessary, but not sufficient condition, for economic growth, what policies would stimulate regional employment growth? The ability to grow new businesses, and therefore the economy, depends on a set of institutional relationships that are economy wide. They include the relationship between new firms and big businesses, government, universities, and the financial system. This facet of entrepreneurship policy we call supporting policies. Without these supporting polices new firms will find it very difficult if not impossible to grow into large successful firms. Growing firms need to be supported with money, research, people, and customers.

The first aspect of this relationship is about how large and new firms often cooperate more than they compete – large firms feed the fish instead of eating them. There are several ways that established businesses work with new firms to promote their growth. Intel, for example, tries to build markets for its chips by investing in companies that develop new systems and products that will use the chips; it has invested in more than a thousand such startups. Second, once a startup firm has developed a good product, a large firm will often simply buy the startup firm; thus it acquires a complete package of proven technology and expertise. Third, established firms often become major customers of new firms; for example, IBM became the largest customer of Microsoft.

The second aspect of institutional support of new firms is federal government funding. The various programs through which new firms participate in the federal R&D infrastructure is one form of support. The Small Business Innovation Research program, for example, gives new technology firms can get grants for product development research. Also, through established procurement programs new firms can qualify for limited priority in selling goods and services to the government. Many of the programs of the US Small Business Administration (SBA) are designed to reduce costs to small firms or to provide funds for their expansion. The SBA also works to reduce regulatory costs and tax complexities for small firms. Finally, the federal spending on R&D supports research in government labs, large firms, and both state and private universities, all of whom may directly benefit new firms through knowledge spillovers from their staff and from reported results.

The third institution supporting new firms is the American University System. The universities and their staff are a constant source of inspiration and knowledge spillovers for new businesses. The US university system is also highly competitive, with an eye on technology commercialization to benefit both the staff and the university budgets. The Bayh–Dole Act of 1980 further fostered the development of new business ideas from federally funded research, and the transfer of technology from universities to the US economy. The United States benefit greatly from the transfer of technology from universities, as well as the steady flow of highly educated individuals who leave the university system each year.

Finally, the financial system plays an important role in providing the capital for high growth companies. First the venture capital industry invests over $20 billion dollars annually in growing firms. Many of the most successful firms in the United States were funded with equity capital from venture capital firms. Second, the ability to raise large amounts of money in the public equity markets also plays an important role in supporting the growth of new firms, and allows firms to buy out their venture capital investors The very active competition between personal credit card issuers also contributes considerable initial debt funding from entrepreneurs for their new businesses that have not yet established their own credit.

11.5 Entrepreneurship and Social Policy

The final facet of entrepreneurship policy is the issue of equity and justice. It is well known that these issues are at the heart of the survival of any society. The equity issue has two sides. One is equal opportunity for all to participate in the entrepreneurial process: women, minorities, equity in finance, etc. The second issue is one of equity of outcome with respect to wealth creation. This issue lies at the heart of the legitimacy issue for any society. The fundamental issue here is one of the sustainability of an entrepreneurial society and the form of the feedback mechanism of wealth creation on society. We suggest that both aspects of equality – equality of access and equality of outcome – can be addressed through philanthropy, the process by which people and institutions give freely of both their wealth and their time.

Philanthropy has been one of the major aspects of, and keys to, American social and cultural development. When combined, entrepreneurship, and philanthropy become a potent force in explaining the long-run dominance of the American economy. In an entrepreneurial society, much of the new wealth created historically has to be given back to the community to build up the social institutions *that have a positive feedback on future economic development.* This entrepreneurship–philanthropy nexus is what sustains American capitalism over time.

How is this philanthropic behavior explained? There was the partly religious and partly secular sensitivity to human pain and suffering in sixteenth-century England. Doubtless, another important motivating factor was Calvinism, which taught that the rich man is a trustee for wealth, which he disposes for benefit of mankind, as a steward who lies under direct obligation to do Christ's will.

American philanthropists, especially those who have made their own fortunes, create foundations that, in turn, contribute to greater and more widespread economic prosperity. This was Andrew Carnegie's hope when he wrote about "the responsibility of wealth" over a century age that still inspires entrepreneurs today, though they usually express it in teams of a duty to "give something back" to the society that helped make their won success possible. This model of entrepreneurial capitalism, despite the unequal distribution of wealth, with its sharp focus on entrepreneurship and philanthropy should be encouraged.

Much of the new wealth created historically has been given back to the community to build up the great institutions that have a *positive feedback on future economic development.* Rather than constraining the rich through taxes, we should allow the rich to successfully campaign for social change through the creation of opportunity. In the past the fight against slavery had some very wealthy backers. If we shut off the opportunities for wealthy individuals to give back their wealth we will also shut off the creation of wealth, which has far greater consequences for an entrepreneurial society.

11.6   Policy Goals of an Entrepreneurial Society

We have laid out a broad structure for formulation of entrepreneurship policy. Because of the broad sweep of entrepreneurship in society such policies affect four distinct levels of society: (1) the individual agent, (2) the business, (3) the economy, and (4) society as a whole. In the United States the attitudes toward entrepreneurship stem from historical path dependence. These are summarized in Figure 11.1.

	Goals	Targets	Instruments
Agent— Occupational Choice Policies	More Effective Entrepreneurs	Individuals	- **Create awareness** - **Entrepreneurship training** - **Facilitate networks**
Business— Enabling Policies	Continuous Innovation	New Firm Formation	- **Finance** - **Regulatory relief** - **SBIR** - **Science parks** - **Tech commercialization**
Economy— Supporting Policies	Economic Growth	Institutions- Universities Government Corporations	- **R&D** - **Higher education** - **Venture capital**
Society— Social Policies	Equal Opportunity	Wealthy Individuals	- **Philanthropy** - **Taxes** - **Social pressure** - **Legal structure**

Fig. 11.1 The four facets of entrepreneurship policy

The first goal is to have more agents consider the choice of whether to engage in entrepreneurial activity. How many entrepreneurs does an economy need and who should be an entrepreneur? These are questions for which there are no easy answers. However, an entrepreneurial society needs effective entrepreneurs. Occupational choice instruments are primarily long-run investments in higher education, more publicity for successful entrepreneurs, and building tolerance for failure. Short-run policy instruments do not easily influence these.

The second goal is to have continuing innovation in the economy – facilitating its evolution and increasing productivity, using economic knowledge to form new firms that produce new products or services, target new markets, or increase efficiency with new processes. The target of entrepreneurship and the goal of continuing innovation can be influenced by policy instruments at both the national and local levels. A number of programs to enable the translation of new knowledge into new firms have been put into place over the past two decades and proved effective. Promoting technology transfer at universities, stimulating development of local knowledge networks, providing business incubator facilities, and funding applied research are among the many enabling programs that lead to more, and more productive, new firms in an area.

The third goal is to increase economic growth. Policies to support the growth of new firms at by big business, government, finance and academia are crucial for economic growth. These supporting policies are also fairly short run in nature, but they also have some long-run aspects. It is clear the instruments like government venture capital resources, training courses, and R&D funding for small firms have all played an important role in supporting growth of businesses and regions.

Our fourth goal is equal opportunity for all members of society. The reconstitution of wealth and its positive feedback on society plays a central role in the sustaining of an entrepreneurial society. The societal traditions of wealth reconstitution by the wealthy in America have a long history, and they have contributed to the public image of successful entrepreneurs as paragons of society. The policy instruments that would target the reconstitute of wealth in a society do not lend themselves to short-run changes. These are instruments that are rather blunt in the short run. Here we believe tax policy is secondary, and social institutions are far more important, and it is the unwritten rather than the written rules that bite more in relation to issues of wealth. In the United States these instruments were honed over several centuries.

Academic research has only recently begun to consider the importance of entrepreneurial policy. The formulation of entrepreneurship policy needs to be carried out in the context of a broad social vision that pays attention to the longer-term positive feedback effects of entrepreneurial activity on opportunity and pluralism, in addition to the more immediate effects of such activity on local growth. Only in this context can we judge the ultimate success or failure of an entrepreneurship policy.

12

Social Wealth Creation via Experimental Entrepreneurial Philanthropy*

I. C. MacMillan

Governments and philanthropists in the United States and other rich nations spend billions of dollars each year supporting philanthropic causes that attend to the manifold social problems of the world. Some of their efforts – perhaps on the order of hundreds of millions of dollars each year – go toward supporting startup firms and small entrepreneurial businesses, a strategy linked to the belief that the creation and growth of new enterprises fuels the growth of the economy, particularly through employment. To date, however, few people have considered the role that entrepreneurial activity can play beyond improving employment. Based on our research, we contend that such

---

* The concept of Experimental Entrepreneurial Philanthropy originated when the author received the FSF Prize and was thinking about how to best use this windfall. The deployment of funds to seed Societal Wealth Enterprises emerged, and the funds were deployed to creating the Experimental Entrepreneurial Philanthropy program at the Wharton School.

activity can directly confront social problems and create new societal wealth.

This paper reports on the launch, at the Snider Entrepreneurial Research Center (SERC) of a longitudinal research program of social interventions based on Experimental Entrepreneurial Philanthropy. Experimental Entrepreneurial Philanthropy is the use of philanthropy to create experimental entrepreneurial firms that attack social problems. Specifically the program focuses on using entrepreneurial experiments to attack health problems in Africa, but success of these pilot programs will be the seeds for expansion to other developing economies.

Before discussing the specific Societal Wealth Enterprises we researched, let us first begin with a review of how, other than job creation, entrepreneurship creates societal wealth.

Productivity enhancement: Many entrepreneurial efforts result in significant enhancement of productivity, often starting at the regional level and then extending to the national level. The creation of Sun Microsystems for instance, massively increased the productivity of engineers, scientists, project managers, and researchers, firdst in the United States, then globally.

National competitiveness: At an aggregate level, the cumulative effects of entrepreneurial activity add to a nation's ability to compete with other nations.

Quality of life: Many entrepreneurs, particularly in the United States, are seizing upon opportunities to create business ventures that focus on improving consumers' quality of life. This enhancement of quality of life manifests itself in several major forms:

- *Enhanced national health* in the form of better ways to treat, diagnose, and prevent illness via products that promote improved wellness and life extension and vastly superior devices for the physically and mentally disadvantaged.
- *Improvements in quality of work life* created by the development of new products and equipment that increase worker safety as well as allow employees more flexibility to work out of their homes or from remote locations.

- *Enhanced national education, training, and learning* using technologies that dramatically improve the quality of the workforce, with concomitant gains in national productivity.
- *Enhanced efficiency of government services* in which entrepreneurial providers of information and telecommunication systems dramatically increase the quality and availability of services.
- *Personal wealth creation leading to philanthropy.* Entrepreneurial success often positively influences societies by creating philanthropists, whose huge infusions of philanthropic funds into areas like the arts (Guggenheim/Getty Museums); medical research (Mayo Clinic, Bill and Melinda Gates Foundation); and social welfare (Turner Foundation) provide critical resources that the public sector either cannot provide or cannot adequately support.

12.1 Societal Wealth Creation through Experimental Entrepreneurial Philanthropy

Coupling this last societal wealth benefit (philanthropy) with the other benefits of entrepreneurial activity creates an opportunity to deploy entrepreneurship research in a radically new way. We can deploy philanthropic seed funds to create entrepreneurial "experiments" to conceive of, plan for, and create enterprises that are designed to profitably attack social problems. In doing so, Societal Wealth Enterprises can serve as an alternative to current ineffective and enormously wasteful public sector initiatives.

The basic thesis is that many social problems, if looked at through an entrepreneurial lens, create opportunity for someone to launch a business that generates profits by alleviating the social problem. In essence, it is a shift in activity from the public domain – governments and non-governmental organizations – to the private domain – businesses and private individuals. This sets in motion a virtuous cycle: the entrepreneur is indented to generate more profits and in so doing, the more profits made, the more the problem is alleviated.

Oftentimes this process is obstructed by two major obstacles: low profitability and the resultant lack of seed funding. This is where the entrepreneurial philanthropist comes in. If philanthropists endow the seed funding for Societal Wealth Enterprises, in many economies, particularly developing ones, it should be possible to attract local entrepreneurs who are quite happy to live with the smaller profit streams eschewed by their counterparts in more wealthy economies. A powerful appeal to the philanthropists is that their contributions have a chance to remove problems rather than to simply alleviate them, and the associated recurrent "annual tin cup" dependencies.

Ideally, the injection of seed funds into pilot entrepreneurial projects will set in motion the first entrepreneurial business, which, if successful, plants the seed for followon entrepreneurial initiatives.

Like all entrepreneurial efforts, however, success is not guaranteed. In fact the cynic might argue that if there were an obvious entrepreneurial solution, an entrepreneur would already have found it! This is where the third component of Experimental Entrepreneurial Philanthropy kicks in. Our position is that we may be able to mobilize the talents of universities and business to undertake a new mode of research via entrepreneurial experimentation – to conceive of, design, and plan Societal Wealth Enterprises and then recruit local entrepreneurs to launch and manage them for the profits they can make, which though small by developed economy standards,can be perfectly adequate by the local entrepreneur's standards.

Experimental Entrepreneurial Philanthropy is already being undertaken by the SERC. Below we describe four major programs at the Experimental Entrepreneurial Philanthropy Program at Wharton. The Program has conceived of possible social entrepreneurial solutions, developed business plans and then seeded the formation of a pilot business to implement the solution as a social experiment, learning and redirecting the pilot business that emerges as reality unfolds the real opportunity.

12.1.1   HIV/AIDS Program

Goal: Increasing the lifespan and employment vitality of AIDS-infected workers.

When large percentages of populations are infected by AIDS, this hollows out and debilitates the workforce, and when large numbers of skilled workers are debilitated it becomes economically important for employers to be able to put in place treatment programs which identify the treatment regimens for diversely affected worker groups.

12.1.1.1 Botswana

Botswana is a country of some 600,370 square kilometers with a population of approximately 1,561,973 (2004 estimates). Four decades of uninterrupted civilian leadership, progressive social policies, and significant capital investment have created one of the most dynamic economies in Africa. However, the nation's impressive economic gains are threatened by one of the world's highest known rates of HIV/AIDS infection. There are an estimated 350,000 people living with the disease, and already 69,000 AIDS orphans; a number that is rapidly climbing. Approximately 5500 babies will be infected with the virus this year alone. Life expectancy at birth is currently 30.76 years (2004 estimates). Without AIDS it would be an estimated 72.4 years.

Facing the epidemic   Botswana is at the forefront of the fight against HIV/AIDS, with one of Africa's most progressive and comprehensive programs for dealing with the disease. In response to the overwhelming number of infections and the critical shortage of physicians, the Ministry of Health has recently made a decision to develop alternative staffing capabilities in the provision of managing anti-retroviral therapy and monitoring patients.

To this end, the Ministry of Health has authorized SERC and the Medical School of the University of Pennsylvania to conduct trials of an HIV-specific patient record monitoring and reporting system with built in decision support tools that in the long run will allow nurses, assisted by the software/database/data mining functionality being introduced by our entrepreneurial software firm, to deliver diagnostic and prescriptive services to vastly more HIV patients. If successful this enterprise will be expanded to the rest of Africa and then the rest of the developing world.

In February 2005 the software was experimentally introduced by SERC into the nation's largest private sector anti-retroviral center, based in Gaberone. As of April 26, 2005 the following progress had been made:

- 3042 patients records have been entered into the system.
- Full electronic laboratory integration is near completion (a first for the country).
- The clinic IT network is made robust and stable.
- The clinic server is accessible from the United States and Europe via broadband radio satellite link.
- Two physicians are already entering complete new patient files while using the system.
- Reception staff and nurses are entering relevant data as patients flow through the clinic.
- The chief physician at the hospital is beginning to identify patients for treatment by two nurses identified as the first non-physician personnel to use the system.

The Medical School of the University of Pennsylvania, The chief physician and her staff at Princess Marina Hospital (the largest ARV distribution point in the world) will support the trials with a view to a full implementation at Princess Marina and later into the national program.

It is our intention to assist the entrepreneurial software provider to implement the software at two smaller government sites in Gaberone as soon as additional funds permit.

12.1.1.2   South Africa

Accounting for 45% of the sub-Saharan GDP,[1] South Africa serves as the financial epicenter of Sub-Saharan Africa. Therefore, when the infection rate in South Africa surpassed 11 percent and the country's life expectancy rate dropped by 35 years, HIV went from a mere problem to a civic, social, and economic crisis. Worse still, the

---

[1] "Africa's Engine", *The Economist*, A survey of Sub-Saharan Africa, January 17, 2004.

government, police, military, nursing, and teaching communities are among the groups with the highest rate of HIV prevalence. Given these warning signs, the necessity for collective action has never been more pressing. The loss of human life on such a scale is not only a human tragedy, but also a prospective catalyst for the downward, irreversible spiral of the South African economy into an unsustainable financial state.

Due to restricted resources and the South African government's somewhat controversial views on HIV/AIDS, over the course of the past 5 years the costs of treatment have largely fallen on South Africa's private sector. Although significant strides in interventions have been made by large multinationals, small- and medium-sized enterprises (SMEs), which employ approximately 55 percent of South African labor, have few, if any, programs in place. This is despite the fact that a quarter of all medium-sized enterprises have reported a tangible erosion of profits due to HIV/AIDS infections.[2] Indeed, studies have calculated the direct costs of an HIV-infected employee to a company as high as 60 percent of the employee's salary.[3] A number of impediments have limited SMEs' ability to provide HIV/AIDS services to their employees. Boston University's Center for International Health and Development explored why, by interviewing 25 South African SMEs that do not provide HIV/AIDS services. The reasons most commonly listed for not providing an HIV/AIDS intervention program are:

(a) a lack of information and access to services,
(b) a low willingness to pay,
(c) a reaction to the stigma,
(d) a lack of pressure to act from stakeholders,
(e) unfit delivery models,
(f) limited capacity.[4]

---

[2] South African Business Coalition on HIV/AIDS: The Impact of HIV/AIDS on Selected Business Sectors in South Africa 2004 (BER – Bureau for Economic Research).

[3] S. Rosen *et al.*, "Care and Treatment to Extend the working lives of HIV-positive employees: calculating the benefits to business," *South African Journal of Science* (July 2000), article can be found at: http://www.internationalhealth.org/aids_economics/Papers/Business%20benefits%20of%20care%20and%20treatment%20(SAJS).pdf

[4] P. Connelly,. "Can small and medium sized enterprises provide HIV/AIDS services to their employees? Constraints and opportunities." Center for International Health and

Our research validates these factors. Accordingly, the proposed intervention model developed at SERC plans to overcome these obstacles by enabling SMEs to participate in a network of subscribing firms sending their workers to a network of clinics, with an entrepreneurial database manger acting as the informational hub between multiple firms and clinics. The software and data management systems are to be based on South Africa's most successful, already proven, clinical practices, but modified for SMEs. The necessary partners and test location have been secured.

12.1.2 Livestock Feed Production

Goal: Increasing the quality and production of livestock in emerging economies.

Application of advanced mathematical techniques like linear programming solutions to the optimal feed mix problem is currently inaccessible to small-scale producers of feedstock for animals bred for meat. A consulting service that uses a highly simplified stripped-down version of more sophisticated programming, which also incorporates data about locally available feed components, has been developed by SERC and launched in Zambia by a local entrepreneurial firm assisted by SERC.

The cost optimization software application was deployed in northern Zambia in November 2003. After a full year of use the beneficiary reported the following:

- Large competitors have been obliged to match the entrepreneur's across-the-board 20 percent selling price reduction in the region.
- Consequentially feeds are now available to a large number of small-scale producers.
- The producer has doubled sales.
- Net margins have increased by between 7 and 10 percent.
- Animal yield and health has increased considerably.

Development, Boston University School of Public Health, Presentation for the African-Asian Society, April 21, 2004.

- Livestock throughput has accelerated, allowing poultry growers another full production cycle per annum (with the same facilities).
- Quality of the meat has improved, with more protein and less fat.

If current success is continued over the test period SERC will be able to roll this out to other emerging economies.

12.1.3 Peanut Processing Plant

Goal: Introducing low-cost, mechanical peanut distribution, collection, and processing plants.

Peanuts provide about 40 percent of all the proteins, carbohydrates, and fats needed for human nutrition. Supplemented with milk this product can virtually replace meat.

The difficulty is that processing of peanuts by hand is enormously time-consuming, and modern processing plants have thus far required very large capital outlays.

What is needed is cheaper, robust processing plants to encourage the farming of peanuts in more remote areas where it currently could be done, but is not done for the above reasons.

Such plants would become a viable source of income in rural agricultural communities. Research shows that women in rural agricultural communities can earn higher wages working in such plants than manually cleaning produce, the other main source of work for women in these areas. Evidence suggests that women use this increase in income to school their children, and sometimes themselves. In addition, peanuts are an important source of food in poorer communities.

The Experimental Entrepreneurial Philanthropy team at SERC undertook it's a research project looking at the peanut industry in South Africa, which has grown at an average CAGR of 4–6 percent per annum for the past 10 years to the current level of about $390 million, with the current tonnage of imported and exported material totaling approximately 130,000 tons. SERC then began researching processing plant of different types and found an established entrepreneurial firm that has developed a robust, low-cost model for purchasing and processing of peanuts, the Kalinda Trading Company. Kalinda has developed customized processing machinery that enables the business to compete with substantially lower capital costs than other commercially available, often imported, machinery.

SERC believes that the Kalinda model can be successfully expanded to regions in Sub-Saharan Africa, Latin America, and Asia. It is estimated that each plant will initially employ 30 to 50 employees, and once fully operational, 80 full-time staff.

The baseline roll-out model entails three phases:

Phase 1: Establish local depots for resale of Kalinda manufactured products.

Phase 2: Establish limited selection and manufacturing facilities to sort, clean, and pack bulk material and to manufacture bulk volumes of peanut butter for the local/regional markets.

Phase 3: Coordinate with local farmers to promote the growing of peanuts for use in the newly established manufacturing plant.

SERC has recruited local entrepreneurs to launch and manage the franchise model. These local entrepreneurs are currently in the process of finalizing the business plan.

12.2   Expansion to other developing economies

The projects undertaken by the Experimental Entrepreneurial Philanthropy Program at SERC have focused so far primarily on Africa, primarily because of our staff's strong regional knowledge and because problems of AIDS and starvation are worst in that part of the world. Our vision, however, is to take these successes to every part of the world with similar problems – Asia, Latin America, the Caribbean – and wherever else there are populations at risk.

12.3 Experimental Entrepreneurial Philanthropy in Developed Economies

Lest it be construed that Experimental Entrepreneurial Philanthropy is confined to developing economies only, SERC is monitoring opportunities in advanced economies as well.

12.3.1 IT and Electronic Equipment Productivity

Goal: Improving electronic equipment efficiency and reducing costs.

In most developed economies IT and other electronic equipment costs are skyrocketing. An entrepreneurial experiment is underway with a startup that will allow remote diagnosis and servicing of high-cost capital equipment and operating systems, like mainframes, centralized servers or NMR/CAT scanning machines. This could result in an overall *national* improvement in the productivity of as much as 2 percent for these systems, and at much lower costs. In this case the SERC role was confined to the provision of advice, guidance and network connections to the entrepreneur. Once the key applications have been prototyped it is SERC's intention to assist in the rapid globalization of the business.

12.3.2 Environmental Protection

Goal: Finding alternatives to landfills for disposing of plastic refuse.

SERC group has been studying an enterprise that physically combines polystyrene (plastic containers) with polyethylene (plastic bags) in a unique way, creating a very strong, rigid, and corrosionless plastic "alloy" material that can be used to build permanent structures. This material can also be reground and used over and over once its original use has been exhausted. The company recently profitably built a small bridge using 200,000 plastic containers – and there are an estimated 40,000 bridges in the United States alone that are in need of replacement.

12.4 Summary

How do we help the world's poor? Handouts seem to have failed. In fact, the 2005 G8 Summit is focused on debt relief, a sign that financial aid has not been as successful as originally hoped. Perhaps the idea behind the proverb – give a man a fish and he soon goes hungry, teach him to fish and he eats forever – represents a viable option in today's world. We believe that business, particularly entrepreneurial endeavors, have a clear role in alleviating societal woes, yet the costs involved are often too high for the average entrepreneur to undertake.

In response to this SERC is doing experimental research along the lines of "Experimental Entrepreneurial Philanthropy," where philanthropists fund research – conducted by universities like Penn – into companies that in making profits also alleviate social ills.

Once the university researchers have identified potential business opportunities – like the peanut processing plant – that can be applied in other countries, the philanthropists will once again help out by funding pilot programs that will eventually pave the way for larger-scale roll-outs. With these foundations in place, local entrepreneurs can pick up the ball and run. Ideally these projects will spark other businesses, starting a cycle that will do more than simply create jobs, but rather help increase the social wealth of a society.

13

Reflections on Public Policy on Entrepreneurship and SMEs

D. J. Storey

13.1 Public Policy on Entrepreneurship and SMEs in Recent Years

I was the 1998 winner of the FSF Nutek Award and this invitation to provide a forward-look encouraged me to go back to review my citation. Of course, as a prize-winner, one never knows why it is that one is selected, but perhaps the citation offers some guidance. It refers to "policy makers" and to "policy relevance" on more than one occasion, and my interpretation is that this stems primarily from a book that I wrote and which was published in 1994 called *Understanding the Small Business Sector*.

Since 1994 my, very subjective, impression is that there has been a substantial increase in interest among academics and public policy makers in the role of new and small enterprises. For example, there have been a number of evaluation studies conducted upon policy instruments and published in good journals, such as *Journal of Business, Entrepreneurship and Regional Development, Scottish Journal of Political Economy,* etc.[1]

Secondly the work by Lundstrom and Stevenson (2001, 2005) *Entrepreneurship Policy, Theory and Practice* has provided a wide-ranging review of entrepreneurship policy in developing countries. It also made the important distinction between entrepreneurship policy, which is focused on individuals, compared with SME policy which is focused on enterprises.

Another indication of the importance of policy is a UK study (Treasury, 2000), which examined and quantified the total amount of taxpayers money distributed by a wide range of government departments seeking to support small businesses. Although the sums from many of the individual organizations/departments are modest, when all of these "pots" were added together, the total expenditure was approximately £8 billion. To place this in some sort of context, the UK spends approximately £7 billion on its police force. Despite this vast expenditure of public funds on small business support, it remains the case that there is no central organization with the task of ensuring value for money from these funds.

13.2   Is Public Policy Important?

Despite these developments it was salutary to receive a (very polite) response from the Editor of the *Journal of Business Venturing* in 2003. David Audretsch, Denny Dennis, and I suggested that a special issue of *JBV* be devoted to public policy toward SMEs. Maybe, after all, the subject was not really of wide interest to scholars of enterprise.

My first reaction was whether this decision reflected a specific US focus of the journal. Some justification for this was provided in a simple diagram taken from Dennis Jr. (2004). It shows that countries varied in their public policy stance toward smaller firms along two dimensions. On the vertical axis was the extent to which they focused on regulation,

---

[1] See Lerner, Lambrecht and Pirnay (2005), Roper and Hewitt-Dundas (2001).

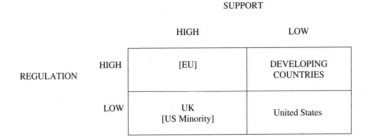

Fig. 13.1

reflected most clearly in the ease or difficulty, in terms of time and cost, of starting a business. Broadly the United States was an exemplar in terms of minimizing regulation, with this being reflected in the work of Djankov *et al.*[2] On the horizontal dimension was the scale of "support" provided for new and small firms. This "support" was normally in the form of taxpayers' money distributed by public organisations either in "hard" or "soft" forms. The United States was perceived by Dennis to spend relatively little public money in this format, although the evidence for this is much more mixed, with even Dennis recognizing that the focus on programmes for "minorities" meant that there was clear exceptions, even in the United States.

In terms of Figure 13.1 therefore the United States is a country where its mainstream small business policy focuses on low regulation and low levels of support. An implicit assumption in the United States might be that enterprise happens naturally and so policies to promote enterprise are unnecessary. However, even this seems to have been challenged, since recent work by Hart (2003), and Holtz-Eakin and Rosen (2004), has shown there is interest in the topic, at least among US economists and political scientists.

Nevertheless Figure 13.1 does make it clear that the US approach is radically different from almost that of all other countries, with most EU countries favouring an approach which is diametrically opposed to the United States. While EU countries are generally reducing their levels

---

[2] The work showed that out of 85 countries examined, the cost of starting a business in the United States was the lowest of all.

of regulation, these remain markedly higher than in the United States. EU countries however, show little indication of reducing their levels of public "support' for small firms, with countries such as Germany, who are currently experiencing high unemployment increasing their levels of public support for new and small enterprises.[3]

The UK – and New Zealand – adopt again a different combination of approaches, combing low levels of regulation with comparatively generous levels of publicly funded support. Finally, it is clear from the work of Djankov *et al.*, (2002) that, in general, the costs of starting a business are vastly higher in developing countries than elsewhere.

For all these reasons it is therefore clear that, from a policy perspective, the United States is different from almost all other countries. Given that the United States chose to be in the "low support" and "low regulation" box it was perhaps unsurprising that the Editor of the leading US academic journal on entrepreneurship did not give a high priority to the subject of policy toward SMEs.

13.3   But What about Outside the United States?

Figure 13.1 emphasizes the point that, while interest in public policy on entrepreneurship and small businesses may generate little interest in the United States, it is very important elsewhere. The scale of taxpayers; money spent on this area is not trivial, but it is rarely quantified.

As noted earlier, a notable exception was a study in the UK by H.M. Treasury (2000). The Treasury showed that the annual budget of the UK Small Business Service (SBS), was almost £400 million annually. To the casual observer, SBS was the main provider of public funds for the advice and financial assistance to small firms in Britain. However, the Treasury study sought to examine *all* public funds which were either spent by government departments or where subsidiaries or tax relief were provided to small firms. When *all* funds were included, total public

---

[3] See, e.g. the Ich-AG programme in Germany which offers interest free subsidies to the unemployed wishing to start a business. A helpful review of these programmes is provided by Bergman and Sternberg (2005).

funds amounted to virtually £8 billion.[4] To place this in context, it meant that there was more taxpayers' money spent on small firms than on the Police Force. It also was clear that there was – and continues to be – no central decision-making body responsible for this £8 billion. Instead, the spending emerges from a massive range of government national/regional departments and local organisations and quasi public bodies.

To my knowledge no comparable study has been undertaken in any other countries but, if it were, I suspect it would yield very similar results – that is expenditure is very much higher than expected and that it lacks co-ordination and coherence.

13.4 So, Is This an Important Area for Future Research?

For all the above reasons I believe the topic of public policy toward enterprise and entrepreneurship to be of massive importance for taxpayers, small business owners, potential entrepreneurs, policy makers, and scholars.

The perspective of taxpayers is rarely addressed in these matters but, since it is their funds that are being provided, it is appropriate to give them the highest priority. Quite simply there is insufficient good research on evaluating whether public funds on enterprise have their desired effect. It is to be hoped that the OECD Ministerial Declaration in Istanbul in 2004 for the need for more high quality evaluation of SME policies is widely implemented.

From the perspective of small business owners, research which examines the combination of regulation and support which they view appropriate for the development of their business is of some value. However, my perspective is that this research is of limited value since owners are imperfectly informed about the available range of options. This is even more the case for potential entrepreneurs, and yet this type of work does appear quite frequently in academic journals.

---

[4] Examples of such expenditure include tax measures to assist such firms such as Venture Capital Trust, lower rates of corporation tax, R&D tax credits and the Enterprise Investment Schemes. These alone cost the UK taxpayer £2.6 billion.

The key target market for public policy research is policy-makers and politicians. These individuals decide public spending priorities and the tax/spend ratio. In practice, they are strongly influenced by the views of small business owners who, almost without exception, seek to minimise regulation. Politicians are also influenced by public servants who, all else equal, may favour public programmes. Our task as scholars is to be a powerful third force in creating an economic environment in which enterprise is facilitated, but in a cost-effective manner.

There is therefore, in principle, a "market" for independent objective and external advice on policy impact and here the contribution of scholars could be considerable. The reality is that, while there has been some valuable work on assessing SME and entrepreneurship policy effectiveness, it is the case that the sophistication of the approaches has been significantly less than, for example, in labour market policies. Take just one example – the impact of publicly provided business advice on small business performance. This is clearly influenced by the types of firms that seek that advice leading to the strong likelihood of "selection bias". Taking this into account is standard practice in labour market studies, whereas this is rare in SME and entrepreneurship policy evaluations, even those which appear in "good" journals.[5]

13.5   But Is the Future Bright?

However the enterprise public policy research areas has recently been stimulated by the contribution of Djankov *et al.* (2002). This work examined the cost of starting a business in 85 countries and linked this to economic development. It concluded that those countries where the costs of business startups were highest were more likely to be poor, corrupt, and undemocratic. They implied that countries where it was easy to start a business were prosperous.

This research has already had considerable influence. Many EU countries, and the European Commission itself, have sought to lower the costs and time of starting a business in the expectation that

---

[5] For a helpful review see Heckman (2001).

this will yield benefits in terms of enterprise and ultimately economic performance.

However, like much good research, the Djankov *et al.* research raises as many questions as it answers. Setting aside the issue of correlation and causation, the fundamental issue is whether making it more difficult to start a business has economic consequences. For example, it may simply convert enterprise from the "observed" economy to the "unobserved." It is also likely, as shown in Figure 13.1, that increases in support can compensate for increases in regulation and produce a more desirable final outcome. The research I am currently undertaking with colleagues in England and Spain, which have very different regulatory environments, suggests that it is the similarities, rather than the differences in new firms in these economies that is the most striking.[6]

13.6 OVERALL

Public policy toward SMEs is important. Those formulating policy do need the help of the research community in creating an environment in which enterprise can thrive. Taxpayers also need to be reassured that they are getting value for their money. The research opportunities are enormous.

---

[6] Capelleras *et al.* (2005).

References

Acs, Z. J. and D. B. Audretsch (1988), 'Innovation in large and small firms: An empirical analysis'. *American Economic Review* **78**(4), 678–690.

Acs, Z. J. and D. B. Audretsch (1990), *Innovation and Small Firms*. Cambridge: MIT Press.

Acs, Z. J., D. B. Audretsch, P. Braunerhjelm, and B. Carlsson (2004), 'The missing link: The knowledge filter and entrepreneurship in endogenous growth'. *Centre for Economic Policy Research (CEPR) Discussion Paper*.

Aldrich, H. E. and T. Baker (2005), 'Blinded by the cites? Has there been progress in entrepreneurship research?'. In *Entrepreneurship 2000*, D. L. Sexton and R. W. Smilor (eds.), pp. 377–400. Chicago, IL: Upstart Publishing Company.

Audretsch, D. B. (1995), *Innovation and Industry Evolution*. Cambridge: MIT Press.

Audretsch, D. B. and M. P. Feldman (1996), 'R&D spillovers and the geography of innovation and production'. *American Economic Review* **86**(3), 630–640.

Audretsch, D. B., M. Keilbach, and E. Lehmann (2005), *Entrepreneurship and Economic Growth*. New York: Oxford University Press.

Audretsch, D. B. and P. E. Stephan (1996), 'Company-scientist locational links: The case of biotechnology'. *American Economic Review* **86**(3), 641–652.

Baker, T. and H. E. Aldrich (1994), 'Friends and strangers: early hiring practices and idiosyncratic jobs'. In *Frontiers of Entrepreneurship Research*, W. Bygrave *et al.* (ed.), pp. 75–87. Center for Entrepreneurial Studies, Babson College, Wellesley, MA.

Baker, T. and H. E. Aldrich (2001), 'The trouble with gurus: responses to dependence and the emergence of employment practices in entrepreneurial firms'. In *Frontiers of Entrepreneurship Research 1999*, P. Reynolds *et al.* (ed.), pp. 1–14. Center for Entrepreneurial Studies, Babson College, Wellesley, MA.

Becattini, G. (1975), 'Invito ad una rilettura di Marshall'. In *Economia della produzione*, A. M. P. Marshall (ed.). Italian translation from the second edition (1881) of *The Economics of Industry*, ISEDI, Milano.

Becattini, G. and F. Musotti, 'Measuring the district effect. Reflections on the literature'. In *Industrial Districts: A new Approach to Industrial Change*, G. Becattini (ed.), Cheltentam, E. Elgar.

Bergman, R. and R. Sternberg (2005), 'How to explain start-up activities from a regional perspective'. In *Empirical Evidence from German Regions*. Paper presented at 2nd GEM Conference, Budapest, May 26–27.

Berle, A. A. and G. Means (1932), *The Modern Corporation and Private Property*. New York: Macmillan.

Berlin, I. (1953/1993), *The Hedgehog and the Fox: An Essay on Tolstoy's View of History*. Chicago: Ivan R. Dee Publisher.

Busenitz, L., G. P. West III, D. Shepherd, T. Nelson, G. N. Chandler, and A. Zacharakis, 'Entrepreneurship emergence: Fifteen years of entrepreneurship research in management journals'. *Journal of Management* **29**(3), 285–308.

Capelleras, J. L., K. Mole, F. G. Greene, and D. J. Storey (2005), 'Do more heavily regulated economies have poorer performing new firms? — Evidence from England and Spain'. CSME Working Paper, Warwick Business School.

Chandler, A. (1977), *The Visible Hand: The Managerial Revolution in American Business*. Belknap Press: Cambridge.

Church, R. (ed.) (1980), *The Dynamics of Victorian Business*. London: Allen and Unwin.

Coleman, J. C. (1988), 'Social capital in the creation of human capital'. *American Journal of Sociology* **94**, S95–S120.

Cooke, T. W. (1841), *Notes of a Tour in the Manufacturing Districts of Lancashire*. London: Duncan and Malcolm.

Cournot, A. A. (1938). *Recherces sur les principes mathématique de la théorie des richesses*, Paris.

Dardi, M. (1984), *Il giovane Marshall. Accumulazione e mercato*. Bologna: Il Mulino.

Davidsson, P. and J. Wiklund (2001), 'Levels of analysis in entrepreneurship research: Current research practices and suggestions for the future'. *Entrepreneurship Theory and Practice* **25**(4), 81–100.

Davis, M. S. (1971), 'That's interesting! Towards a phenomenology of sociology and a sociology of phenomenology'. *Philosophy of the Social Sciences* **1**, 309–344.

Dennis Jr., W. J. (2004), 'Creating and sustaining a viable small business sector'. Paper presented at School of Continuing Education, University of Oklahoma, October 27.

Djankov, S., R. L. Porta, F. L. de Silanes, and A. Schleifer (2002), 'The regulation of entry'. *Quarterly Journal of Economics* **CXVII**(1), 1–37.

Duchesneau, D. A. and W. B. Gartner (1990), 'A profile of new venture success and failure in an emerging industry'. *Journal of Business Venturing* **5**(5), 297–312.

Frank, R. H. and P. J. Cook (1995), *The Winner Take All Society*. New York: Free Press.

Frey, B. S. and M. Benz (2003), 'Being Independent is a great thing: subjective evaluations of self-employment and hierarchy'. CESifo Working Paper, No. 959.

Galbraith, J. K. (1956), *American Capitalism*. Boston: Houghton Mifflin.

Gartner, W. B. (1985), 'Did River City really need a boy's band?'. *New Management* **3**(1), 28–34.

Gartner, W. B. (1987), 'A pilgrim's progress'. *New Management* **4**(4), 4–7.

Gartner, W. B. (1990a), 'To live: The obligation of individuality. A review of the film Ikiru, directed by Akira Kurosawa'. *The Organizational Behavior Teaching Review* **14**(2), 138–143.

Gartner, W. B. (1990b), 'What are we talking about when we talk about entrepreneurship?'. *Journal of Business Venturing* **5**(1), 15–28.

Gartner, W. B. (1993a), 'Can't see the trees for the forest. A review of the film *The Man Who Planted Trees*, directed by Frederick Back'. *Journal of Management Education* **17**(2), 269–274.

Gartner, W. B. (1993b), 'Words lead to deeds: Towards an organizational emergence vocabulary'. *Journal of Business Venturing* **8**(3), 231–240.

Gartner, W. B. (2001), 'Is there an elephant in entrepreneurship? Blind assumptions in theory development'. *Entrepreneurship Theory and Practice* **25**(4), 27–39.

Gartner, W. B. (2004), 'Achieving 'critical mess' in entrepreneurship scholarship'. In *Advances in Entrepreneurship, Firm Emergence, and Growth*, J. A. Katz and D. Shepherd (eds.), Vol. 7, pp. 199–216. Greenwich, CT: JAI Press.

Gartner, W. B. and S. Birley (2002), 'Introduction to the special issue on qualitative methods in entrepreneurship research'. *Journal of Business Venturing* **17**(5), 387–395.

Gartner, W. B., T. R. Mitchell, and K. H. Vesper (1989), 'A taxonomy of new business ventures'. *Journal of Business Venturing* **4**(3), 169–186.

Gartner, W. B., K. G. Shaver, N. M. Carter, and P. D. Reynolds (2004), *Handbook of Entrepreneurial Dynamics: The Process of Business Creation*. Thousand Oaks, CA: Sage Publications.

Gartner, W. B., J. A. Starr, and S. Bhat (1999), 'Predicting new venture survival: An analysis of 'anatomy of a startup cases from *Inc. Magazine*'. *Journal of Business Venturing* **14**, 215–232.

Groenewegen, P. (1995). *A Soaring Eagle. Alfred Marshall, 1842–1924*, Edward Elgar, Brookfield.

Groenewegen, P. (ed.) (1996), *Official Papers of Alfred Marshall. A Supplement*. Cambridge: CUP.

Hamilton, B. H. (2000), 'Does entrepreneurship pay? An empirical analysis of returns to self-employment'. *Journal of Political Economy* **108**(3), 604–632.

Hart, D. M. (2003), *Emergence of Entrepreneurship Policy: Governance, Start-Ups and Growth of the US Knowledge Economy.* Cambridge University Press.

Hearn, W. E. (1863), *Plutology: Plutology, or the Theory of the Efforts to Satisfy Human Wants.* Melbourne: G. Robertson and Co.

Heckman, J. (2001), 'Accounting for heterogeneity, diversity and general equilibrium in evaluating social programmes'. *Economic Journal* **111**(475), F654–F699.

Hjorth, D., 'Organizational entrepreneurship: With de Certeau on creating heterotopias (or spaces for play)'. *Journal of Management Inquiry.* in press.

Hjorth, D. (2003), *Rewriting Entrepreneurship: For a New Perspective on Organizational Creativity.* Copenhagen: CBS Press.

Holtz-Eakin, D. and H. Rosen (eds.) (2004), *Public Policy and the Economics of Entrepreneurship.* Cambridge, MA: MIT Press.

Jaffe, A. (1989), 'The real effects of academic research'. *American Economic Review* **79**, 957–970.

Jha, N. (1973), *The Age of Marshall. Aspects of British Economic Thought 1890–1915.* London: Frank Cass.

Katz, J. (2005). http://eweb.slu.edu/welcome.htm.

Katz, J. and W. B. Gartner (1988), 'Properties of emerging organizations'. *Academy of Management Review* **13**(3), 429–442.

Keynes, J. M. (ed.) (1926), *Official Papers by Alfred Marshall.* London: Macmillan.

Kim, P. H. and H. E. Aldrich (2005), 'Fruits of co-laboring: Effects of entrepreneurial team stability on the organizational founding process'. Paper presented at the *Babson Conference on Entrepreneurship*, Babson College.

Lambrecht, J. and F. Pirnay (2005), 'An evaluation of public support measures for private external consultancies to SMEs in the Walloon Region of Belgium'. *Entrepreneurship and Regional Development* **17**(2), 89–108.

Landstrom, H. (2005), *Pioneers in Entrepreneurship*. New York, NY: Springer Science and Business Media, Inc.

Langer, E. J. (1979), *The Power of Mindful Learning*. Cambridge, MA: Perseus Publishing.

Lerner, J., 'The government as venture capitalist — The long run impact of the SBIR programme'. *Journal of Business* **72**(3), 285–318.

Lincoln, Y. S. and E. G. Guba (1985), *Naturalistic Inquiry*. Beverly Hills, CA: Sage Publications.

Lipset, S. M. and R. Bendix (1959), *Social Mobility in Industrial Society*. Berkeley: University of California Press.

Lundstrom, A. and L. Stevenson (2001), *Entrepreneurship Policy for the Future*. Stockholm: FSF.

Lundstrom, A. and L. Stevenson (2005), *Entrepreneurial Policy — Theory and Practice*. Boston: Springer.

Marshall, A. (1919), *Industry and Trade*. London: Macmillan.

Marshall, A. (1961), *Principles of Economics*. Variorum, London: Macmillan, ninth edition. 2 Vols.

Marshall, A. and M. P. (1879), *The Economics of Industry*. London: Macmillan, first edition.

Marshall, M. P. (1947), *What I Remember*. Cambridge, CUP. *Parliamentary Papers 1890*, Report of the Committee appointed to inquire into the Census, London: [Cmnd 6071], LVIII. Minutes of Evidence, pp. 1462–1565.

Pigou, A. C. (ed.) (1925), *Memorials of Alfred Marshall*. London: Macmillan.

Poire, M. and C. Sabel (1984), 'The benefits of Lendign relationships: evidence from small business data'. *Journal of Finance* **49**, 3–37.

Putnam, R. D. (1993), *Making Democracy Work*. Princeton: Princeton University Press.

Pyke, F., G. Becattini, and W. Sengenberger (eds.) (1990), *Industrial Districts and Inter-firm Cooperation in Italy*. IILS, Geneva.

Raffaelli, T. (2003), *Marshall's Evolutionary Economics*. Routledge, London.

Raffaelli, T., E. Biagini, and T. R. McWilliams (eds.) (1995), *Alfred Marshall's Lectures to Women*. Aldershot: E. Elgar.

Reynolds, P. D., W. D. Bygrave, and E. Autio (2003), *Global Entrepreneurship Monitor 2003 Global Report.* Babson College and Ewing Marion Kauffaman Foundation: Babson Prak, MA and Kansas City, MO.

Riesman, D. (1950), *The Lonely Crowd: A Study of the Changing American Character.* New Haven: Yale University Press.

Romer, P. M. (1986), 'Increasing returns and long-run growth'. *Journal of Political Economy* **94**(5), 1002–1037.

Roper, S. and N. Hewitt-Dundas (2001), 'Grant assistance and small firm development in Northern Ireland and the Republic of Ireland'. *Scottish Journal of Political Economy* **48**(1), 99–117.

Ruef, M., H. E. Aldrich, and N. Carter (2003), 'The structure of organizational founding teams: Homophily, strong ties, and isolation among U.S. entrepreneurs'. *American Sociological Review* **68**(2), 195–222.

Sargant, W. L. (1857), *Economy of the Labouring Classes.* London: Simpkin, Marshall and Co.

Singer, M. (2001), 'The book eater'. *The New Yorker* February **5**, 62–71.

Solow, R. (1956), 'A contribution to the theory of economic growth'. *Quarterly Journal of Economics* **70**, 65–94.

Steyaert, C. (1995). Perpetuating entrepreneurship through dialogue. A social constructionist view. Unpublished doctoral dissertation. Katholieke Universiteit Leuven, Department of Work and Organizational Psychology.

Steyaert, C. (1997), 'A qualitative methodology for process studies of entrepreneurship: Creating local knowledge through stories'. *International Studies of Management and Organization* **27**(3), 13–33.

Stinchcombe, A. L. (1965), 'Social structure and organizations'. In *Handbook of Organizations*, J. G. March (ed.), pp. 142–193. Chicago: Rand McNally.

Suedfeld, P. and P. E. Tetlock (2002), 'Individual differences in information processing'. In *Blackwell Handbook of Social Psychology: Intraindividual Processes*, A. Tesser and N. Schwarz (eds.), pp. 284–304. Oxford: Blackwell Publishers.

Tetlock, P. E. (2005), *Expert Political Judgment.* Princeton: Princeton University Press.

Thurow, L. C. (1985), 'Healing with a thousand bandages'. *Challenge* **28**, 1–14.

Treasury, H. M. (2000), *Cross Cutting Review of Government Services for Small Businesses*. London: HMSO.

Weick, K. E. (1979), *The Social Psychology of Organizing*. New York: Random House.

Whitaker, J. K. (1975), *Early Economic Writings of Alfred Marshall*. London: Macmillan. 2 Vols.

Whitaker, J. K. (ed.) (1996), *The Correspondence of Alfred Marshall. Economist*. Cambridge: Cambridge University Press. 3 Vols.

Whyte, W. H. (1960), *The Organization Man*. Hammondsworth, Middlesex: Penguin.

Williamson, O. E. (1968), 'Economies as an antitrust defense: The welfare tradeoffs'. *American Economic Review* **58**(1), 18–36.

Xu, J. C. and H. Aldrich (2005), 'Learning to live with dependence traps: Retention of critical high-skill employees in IT start-ups'. Paper presented at the *Academy of Management Meetings*, Hawaii.